IBM® PC DOS and Microsoft® Windows™ User's Guide

IBM PC DOS and Microsoft Windows User's Guide
Copyright © 1994 by Que® Corporation.

Library of Congress Catalog No.: 94-67256

ISBN: 1-56529-884-5

97 96 95   15 14 13 12 11

Interpretation of the printing code: the rightmost double-digit number is the year of the book's printing; the rightmost single-digit number, the number of the book's printing. For example, a printing code of 94-1 shows that the first printing of the book occurred in 1994.

Screens reproduced in this book were created using Collage Plus from Inner Media, Inc., Hollis, NH.

Trademarks

Acknowledgments

Thanks to the IBM PC DOS team in Boca for its technical review of this book.

Thanks very much to Barb Colter for all her hard work.

Author

Suzanne Weixel

Publisher

David P. Ewing

Associate Publisher

Paul Boger

**Director of Operations
and Editing**

Chris Katsaropoulos

Managing Editor

Sheila B. Cunningham

Senior Editor

Jeannine Freudenberger

Production Editor

Barb Colter

Technical Editor

Rolf A. Crozier

Editorial Coordinator

Elizabeth D. Brown

Book Designer

Paula Carroll

Production Team

Steve Adams
Angela Bannan
Amanda Byers
Anne Dickerson
Karen Dodson
Jenny Kucera
Bob LaRoche
Caroline Roop
Bobbi Satterfield
Michael Thomas
Tina Trettin
Donna Winter
Lillian Yates

Composed in *Stone Serif* and *Courier* by Que Corporation

Contents at a Glance

Table of Contents

4 Making Windows Work   65

Part II Beyond the Basics   127

Introduction

By itself, a computer is just a box and a screen. Ultimately, you are faced with the challenge of bringing it to life. This means mastering the computer's operating system, which is PC DOS.

No matter what you may have heard, PC DOS isn't a hostile environment that only people with advanced degrees in computer engineering can master. PC DOS is a tool that people at all levels use to manage the information that computers store in files.

PC DOS does depend on the keyboard, however, and it does rely on commands that must be typed correctly. Everyone who uses PC DOS is familiar with the message `Bad command or file name` that appears when you mistype a command or file name.

With Windows, you can access the power of PC DOS without committing a single command to memory. You can use a mouse to point and click your way among pictures and plain English words to accomplish disk and file management tasks—without touching a keyboard. When used together, IBM PC DOS and Windows make controlling your computer a pleasure, not a chore.

What Does This Book Contain?

Each chapter in the *IBM PC DOS and Microsoft Windows User's Guide* is built around a set of related tasks. The chapters are organized so that you can use the information they present to accomplish the tasks. In addition, the chapters are grouped into parts. You don't have to read the book sequentially to learn to use IBM PC DOS and Windows 3.1. Feel free to jump around from chapter to chapter and section to section to find the information you want.

From beginning to end, the chapters move from the basics—from under-standing your computer system, to using common PC DOS and Windows commands, and then into more advanced tasks, such as customizing your desktop, configuring your computer, safeguarding your system and data, and compressing your data.

Part I: PC Basics

In Chapter 1, "Understanding System Basics," you are introduced to the hardware and software components of your computer.

In Chapter 2, "Making PC DOS Work," you learn how to use PC DOS to manage your files and disks.

In Chapter 3, "Working with the Windows Desktop," you learn how to start and exit Windows, and how to recognize the different parts of the Windows desktop.

In Chapter 4, "Making Windows Work," you learn how to manage the Windows desktop and how to use the Program Manager to organize your programs.

In Chapter 5, "Using File Manager," you learn to use the Windows File Manager to manage your files and disks.

Part II: Beyond the Basics

In Chapter 6, "Customizing Your Desktop," you learn to set up the Windows desktop to suit your own particular needs.

In Chapter 7, "Working with the Text Editor," you learn to edit ASCII files with the E Editor.

In Chapter 8, "Configuring Your Personal Computer," you explore the different ways you can use the AUTOEXEC.BAT and CONFIG.SYS files to set up your computing environment and how to optimize your computer's memory usage.

In Chapter 9, "Controlling the Printer," you learn how to set up your printer for use in Windows and how to make the most of available fonts and printer drivers.

In Chapter 10, "Using IBM Tools," you learn about using PC DOS to safeguard your hardware and software. The chapter covers the PC DOS utilities—AntiVirus, Backup, Undelete, and Defrag. In addition, you learn about the MSCDEX command, PenDOS, and PCMCIA-based features in this chapter (for users who have a computer equipped with a CD-ROM drive, a PCMCIA memory card, or a pen-based application).

In Chapter 11, "Using Data Compression," you learn what a data compression program does, why users need one, and how to use SuperStor/DS.

In Appendix A, "The PC DOS Top Twenty," is a list of 20 of the most common and useful PC DOS commands.

In Appendix B, "Compatibility Considerations Regarding SuperStor/DS," you learn of items you should review before you begin compressing your data using SuperStor/DS. You should make sure that the programs you are using are compatible with SuperStor/DS.

Who Should Use This Book?

The *IBM PC DOS and Microsoft Windows User's Guide* is a useful book for anyone who wants to get the most from a personal computer that is running both IBM PC DOS and Windows 3.1. Although the book is useful for everyone, it is designed especially for new computer users, casual users, or users who don't need to or want to learn everything about PC DOS and Windows. The book presents enough basic information to get you started if you are a first-time user and then builds on your growing understanding by introducing more advanced topics.

Where to Find More Help

After you master the features in this book, you may want to learn more about the advanced capabilities of PC DOS and Windows. If so, you can turn to Que's *Using Windows 3.1*, Special Edition, which can be purchased from retail stores.

Both PC DOS and Windows provide extensive on-line Help to answer many of your questions. To learn about getting Help with using PC DOS commands, see Chapter 2, "Making PC DOS Work." To learn about getting Help with using Windows, see Chapter 4, "Making Windows Work."

Conventions Used in This Book

This book has certain conventions to help you use and understand the information in this book:

- Keys that you press and text that you type appear in **boldface** type. The text you type is uppercase, although you usually can type either uppercase or lowercase.

- Key combinations, such as **Ctrl+Enter**, indicate that you should press and hold down the first key as you press the second key.

- Important words or phrases appear in *italics* the first time they are discussed.

- Screen displays and messages appear in a `special typeface`.

- Menu commands appear as Choose **F**ile, **R**un. To use these commands, you use the mouse to click the File menu and then click the Run option on that menu. Alternatively, you can press **Alt+F** and then press **R**.

- *Notes* provide information that might help you avoid problems or accomplish some task in a more efficient manner.

- **Keywords** in the margins briefly define new terms that you encounter as you read this book.

- **If you have problems...** paragraphs provide troubleshooting information to help you escape from problem situations.

Part I
PC Basics

Chapter 1

Understanding System Basics

"Using a computer is easy." You've heard that statement before. It's the kind of glib remark that might make you wish for an adding machine and ballpoint pen instead of a computer.

Personal computers are logical. They function according to very strict, straightforward rules and guidelines. All you have to do is learn the rules, and you can take charge of the computer on your desk. Luckily, the application programs written for computers are continually becoming easier to use; the combination of PC DOS and Windows (two pieces of software that are explained in the following section) make learning the rules easier than ever.

With PC DOS and Windows, you can access all the power of your computer. Before you put your computer to work, however, you need to understand its components, and you need to know how they work together. This chapter describes the relationship between personal computer hardware and the operating system.

Understanding Your Computer System

Hardware
The physical parts of the computer that you can see and touch.

All personal computers consist of the same basic *hardware* components:

- *System Unit*. The system unit is the box that holds all the electrical components of your computer, as well as some peripheral devices, such as disk drives and modems.

- *Keyboard*. You use the keyboard to communicate with the computer by typing entries and issuing commands. Computer keyboards are similar to typewriter keyboards; they have all the traditional letter and punctuation keys. Computer keyboards also have special keys such as Alt, Ctrl, Esc, Enter, and the arrow keys.

■ *Display*. The display shows on a screen what you type at the keyboard.

■ *Diskette drive*. The diskette drive (also called the floppy disk drive) is the door into your computer. The computer reads information from and writes information to the diskettes you insert into the drive.

Hard disk

A fixed magnetic device used to store computer files.

■ *Hard disk drive*. The hard disk drive stores the application programs and data files with which you work.

■ *Mouse*. The mouse is a pointing device that enables you to move the mouse pointer on-screen, select objects, and issue commands.

■ *Printer*. The printer makes a paper copy of the data that you create on the computer. To print anything, you need to attach and install a printer.

All computers have the same basic hardware components.

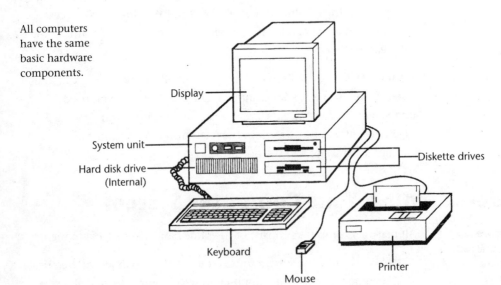

As long as your computer has these main components, the shape and size of your computer does not matter. For example, you can find equally powerful machines in the traditional desktop and tower systems, in floor models, in portable laptop models, or in notebook computers.

Software
Program and data files created, stored, and run by your computer. These terms—applications, software, and programs—are often used interchangeably.

By itself, a computer is just an appliance made of plastic and metal, not so different from a toaster oven. To bring the computer to life, you need *software.*

Software programs designed for use on personal computers fall into two basic types:

- *System software.* Controls the way the different pieces of hardware operate and the way the computer responds to commands. PC DOS and Windows are both examples of system software.

- *Application software.* Enables you to perform specific tasks, such as word processing, desktop publishing, or spreadsheet tasks. Microsoft Word and Lotus 1-2-3 are examples of application software.

Understanding PC DOS

Disk operating system
A system software program that controls the way a computer processes information.

PC DOS (to many computer users, just DOS) is a tool you use to manage the information your computer stores in disk files. DOS stands for *disk operating system.* PC DOS is a collection of programs and standard routines that enable you to communicate with your computer and enable your computer to communicate with hardware devices.

You cannot accomplish anything on your computer without PC DOS. The computer and application programs alone are useless. With PC DOS, however, you can issue commands, start application programs, and manage information.

Interface
A point of communication between you and your computer or between different components of the computer.

With PC DOS, you can interact with your computer through either of two *interfaces*:

- *PC DOS command prompt.* The line in which you can type commands by using precise command syntax. For more information, see the section "Typing PC DOS Commands," later in this chapter.

The PC DOS command prompt, which looks like the following, indicates that PC DOS is waiting for you to enter commands:

```
c:\>
```

After the PC DOS command prompt, you use the keyboard to type the commands.

- *IBM DOS Shell.* A window displaying menus, dialog boxes, and icons that you can use to enter commands. For more information, see the section "Using the IBM DOS Shell," later in this chapter.

In the IBM DOS Shell, you communicate with PC DOS by using the mouse, menu commands, and icons.

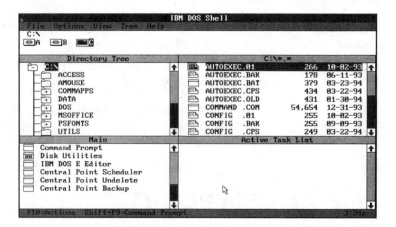

IBM updates PC DOS periodically by adding new commands and making other commands work better. Each time a new version is released, it gets a new number. If the changes are minor, only the number to the right of the decimal point changes. If the changes are significant, the number to the left of the decimal point changes. The most current version is PC DOS 6.3.

Understanding Windows

Graphical user interface

A visual interface that combines graphics, menus, and commands that you use to communicate with your computer.

Microsoft Windows is a *graphical user interface* (GUI) that makes it even easier for you to use PC DOS to communicate with your computer. Windows displays icons, menus, and dialog boxes so that you can see exactly what you are doing and what tools you are using at all times. These displayed elements are defined as follows:

- *Icon.* A small picture used to represent a system component or command on-screen.

- *Menu.* A list of commands.

- *Dialog box.* A window in which you can enter information that PC DOS or another application program needs to continue processing a command (not shown in the following figure).

Windows is a graphical user interface that enables you to communicate with your computer through icons, menus, and dialog boxes.

Menu items

Icons

Inactive window

Active window

The design of Windows is based on the concept that your computer should be like your desktop. With Windows, you can keep many different files and projects available at the same time and switch among them just by reaching for the one you need—as if they were on your desk.

For more information about using Windows, see Chapter 3, "Working with the Windows Desktop," and Chapter 4, "Making Windows Work."

Understanding Disks and Disk Drives

Disk drive
A hardware device that reads from and writes data to magnetic storage disks.

Your computer stores information that is not currently in use on a magnetic storage disk in a *disk drive.* Disk drives are usually installed inside the system unit, although some are attached externally with cables.

There are two basic types of disk drives: *diskette* (or floppy) and hard. Computers can contain more than one disk drive and more than one

Diskette
A removable magnetic device used to store computer files.

disk drive type. Most computers come with at least one hard disk drive and one diskette drive, but different drive combinations are common. For example, your computer can have two diskette drives in addition to one hard drive. If you are connected to a network, your computer may not have a hard disk drive at all.

No matter how many disk drives you have, they follow the same naming scheme: the first diskette drive is named drive A; the second, drive B. The first hard disk is named drive C, and so on.

Diskettes

Diskettes come in two sizes:

     5 1/4-inch

     3 1/2-inch

Each drive uses only one size or the other. If you have a 5 1/4-inch drive, you must use 5 1/4-inch diskettes. If you have a 3 1/2-inch drive, you must use 3 1/2-inch diskettes. Your computer can have both a 5 1/4-inch and a 3 1/2-inch drive.

A 5 1/4-inch diskette fits in a 5 1/4-inch drive.

A 3 1/2-inch diskette fits in a 3 1/2-inch drive.

Capacity
The measure of the amount of data that can be stored on a disk.

Diskettes also come in different *capacities*, which are measured in kilo-bytes (abbreviated *K*) or in megabytes (abbreviated *M*, *MB*, or *meg*). One byte equals approximately one typed character. One kilobyte equals approximately one thousand bytes (1,024 to be exact), and one megabyte equals approximately one million bytes.

The 5 1/4-inch diskettes come in two capacities:

> 360K, double-density diskettes can store about 360,000 characters of information.

> 1.2M, high-density diskettes can store 1.2 million bytes.

The 3 1/2-inch diskettes come in three capacities:

> 720K, double-density diskettes can store about 720,000 characters of information.

> 1.44M, high-density diskettes can store 1.44 million bytes.

> 2.88M diskettes can store 2.88 million bytes.

Format
To prepare a diskette for use by PC DOS.

To prepare a diskette for use, you must *format* it. (Some companies sell preformatted diskettes, however.) Keep in mind that you must format a diskette to the correct capacity. That is, you cannot buy a 360K diskette and then format it as a 1.2M diskette.

Hard Disks

Hard disks can store more information than diskettes store. Each hard disk drive contains many disks, or platters, all of which are used to store data.

A hard disk drive contains many disks, which are used to store data.

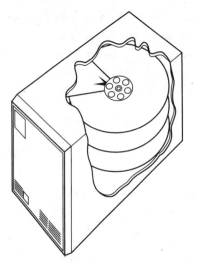

Hard disk capacities are measured in megabytes and come in various sizes: 20M, 30M, 40M, 60M, 80M, 100M, and up.

Hard disks are more durable than diskettes. Hard disks are fixed inside the disk drive, which is usually encased inside the system unit. For this reason, they are not as susceptible to dirt and damage as diskettes.

Average access time
The speed with which a disk drive can find data stored on a disk.

Hard disk drives access information on a disk faster than diskette drives. Most hard drives have *average access times* between 15 and 20 milliseconds.

Understanding Disk Organization

Think about how you store items in your office. You may have a filing cabinet in which you keep folders containing information that pertains to different projects, clients, patients, or some other group—maybe logical, maybe not. Within each folder, you have articles, letters, diagrams, reports—anything you want to save.

Directory
On a disk, a grouping of files and other directories that PC DOS uses to locate data.

PC DOS offers you a similar storage method for keeping track of data. You use a disk the same way you use a filing cabinet. On each disk, you create *directories* that provide the same function as a file folder in a filing cabinet. Within the directories, you store files—the same items you would store in a file folder—such as memos, articles, diagrams, and so on.

Understanding Directory Hierarchy

Directory tree
A diagram showing the organization of directories and files on a disk.

On a disk, the organization of directories is hierarchical, which means that layers of directories grow out of one main directory. Because directories on a disk look like the connected branches of a tree, a diagram of the directories is called a *directory tree*. The main directory, out of which all the other directories grow, is called the *root directory*.

In the PC DOS directory structure, the root directory is the top directory.

Root directory
The main directory on a disk, out of which all other directories grow.

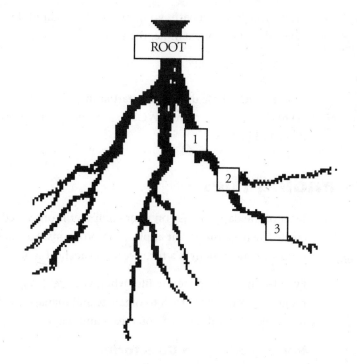

The numbered boxes represent directories on branches of the tree-structured hierarchy.

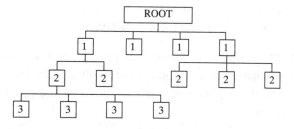

In PC DOS, the root directory is designated by a single backslash (\). To identify a directory other than the root, the backslash is followed by the other directory's name, as in `C:\DOS\DATA`.

Path
The list of directories, starting with the root, that leads to a specific file.

Directories can contain other directories or files. To perform any action or command on a file, you must tell PC DOS exactly where on the directory tree the file is located. To do so, you specify the *path* from the disk drive, referred to as drive A, B, C, and so on. The path specifies the route PC DOS travels to find a file—from the root directory, possibly through several other directories, to the directory that contains the file, and all the way to the file itself.

Subdirectory
Sometimes directories other than the root directory are called *subdirectories*. However, the terms are interchangeable.

When you specify a path, you separate each pair of directory names by a backslash (\). For example, the path

    C:\WORD\REPORTS

gives PC DOS these directions: start at drive C, go from the root directory (\) to the directory named WORD, and then go to the subdirectory named REPORTS.

Understanding Files

File
A collection of data stored as a unit on a disk.

Most of the data you use on your computer is organized into *files*. You create the files using your application programs. For example, every word processing document is a file. Every spreadsheet is also a file, and so on.

Even though you create the files when you are using the application programs, you use PC DOS to organize and manage the files. You must follow PC DOS rules when you create and name files.

Naming Files and Directories

You name files and directories to help you identify their contents and so that PC DOS can find them on a disk.

Extension
A three-letter suffix added to a file name that describes the file's contents.

An entire file name is made up of two parts: the file name, which can be up to eight characters long, and an optional file name *extension*, which can be three characters long. The file name and extension are separated by a period.

As discussed earlier in this chapter, the backslash symbol is used alone to identify the root directory. To identify a directory other than the root, the backslash symbol is followed by a directory name. Directory names, like file names, can be up to eight characters long. Directory names do not usually include extensions.

1

You cannot use these characters in a file or directory name:

' / \ [ ] : ; + = , * ? and ¦ (the vertical bar symbol)

REPORT.DOC is a valid file name. REPORT is the file name, and DOC is the extension. The file name should tell you what the report contains; the extension often tells you the type of file. Some application programs assign an extension automatically.

MY NOTES is not a valid file name because a file name cannot contain spaces. If you want to separate words in a file name, you can use the underline character as in MY_NOTES.

Note: *You should give some thought to file and directory names. Names should clearly identify the contents of the item.*

Within one directory, subdirectories and files must have unique names. However, you can have another subdirectory or file with the same name if it is stored in another directory. For example, you can have a file named MEMO.DOC stored in both the LETTERS subdirectory on drive C, and in the BUDGET directory on drive C. You cannot have two files named MEMO.DOC in the LETTERS subdirectory.

Using Wild Cards

Wild cards
Characters used to represent one or more other characters.

When you want to work with a group of files, you can type *wild cards* within file names in commands given at the PC DOS command prompt. There are two wild cards: the asterisk (*) and the question mark (?).

The question mark wild card (?) is used in place of any single character.

The asterisk wild card (*) is used in place of a single character and all the characters that follow it in a file name or extension—until you type another character.

File spec
An abbreviation for file specification. The complete name and path to a file stored on a disk.

You can use wild cards in different combinations to control which files are included in a group. Suppose that you are writing a book that has eight chapters. The file for each chapter is named CHAP, followed by the chapter number, a period, and the file extension DOC. When you want to copy all the files (CHAP1.DOC through CHAP8.DOC), you can use a *file spec* such as:

CHAP?.DOC

This file spec uses the ? wild card and tells PC DOS to include every file name beginning with *CHAP* and followed by any single character and the *DOC* extension. Remember that each ? wild card represents only one character.

Suppose that your book is 15 chapters long and the files are named CHAP1.DOC through CHAP15.DOC, however, you need to use a different wild card—the asterisk. To copy all the files for this book, you can use a file spec such as

CHAP*.DOC

This file spec tells PC DOS to include every file name beginning with *CHAP*, followed by any number of characters and the *DOC* extension. Remember that the * wild card represents any number of characters.

Special Files

Your computer contains three special files that you should understand:

CONFIG.SYS

AUTOEXEC.BAT

COMMAND.COM

When you first start PC DOS, it looks for a file named AUTOEXEC.BAT. This file must be stored in the root directory. PC DOS finds the file and carries out its instructions. This file can include commands that control different settings you want to use every time you start your computer. For example, you might include a PATH command that tells PC DOS where your application programs are located.

Configuration
The way the hardware and software of a computer is set up or organized.

Another special file that PC DOS uses when it starts is CONFIG.SYS, a *configuration* file. Some application programs require special commands. These commands are contained in the CONFIG.SYS file. Settings in the CONFIG.SYS file control the way PC DOS uses files, memory, application programs, and hardware devices.

To process commands, you must have a file named COMMAND.COM. COMMAND.COM is the command processor. It contains the most commonly used PC DOS commands. When you install PC DOS, this file is copied to the hard drive.

1

When dealing with these special files, keep these rules in mind:

■ Don't delete COMMAND.COM, AUTOEXEC.BAT, or CONFIG.SYS.

■ Don't try to change the contents of COMMAND.COM.

■ As you add application programs to the computer, the documenta-tion may tell you to make changes to the AUTOEXEC.BAT file or the CONFIG.SYS file, or the application program itself may auto-matically make these changes. Be careful when making any changes to these files. You should understand each command in the file before changing anything. Also, it is a good idea to keep a copy of the original versions of these files in case something goes wrong with the new files.

Note: *For more information on the CONFIG.SYS and AUTOEXEC.BAT files, see Chapter 8, "Configuring Your Personal Computer."*

Understanding the IBM DOS Shell

Since Version 5.0, PC DOS has included its own built-in graphical user interface, the IBM DOS Shell. Rather than use the command line to enter commands, you can enter commands through the Shell.

The IBM DOS Shell view is a full-screen graphical window. You can issue most PC DOS commands by using a mouse or the keyboard to point to and select pull-down menus and dialog boxes. You do not have to re-member the names of commands to use the IBM DOS Shell. You just select actions from menus, type answers to questions, and check options in dialog boxes.

The Shell view is the friendliest way to use PC DOS. For example, a direc-tory listing is automatic when you are in the IBM DOS Shell. You always see a listing of the subdirectories and files in the current directory. To start the IBM DOS Shell from the PC DOS command prompt, type **DOSSHELL** and press Enter.

Looking at the IBM DOS Shell

When you start the IBM DOS Shell, you see a full screen. This initial screen contains information that is displayed automatically. The screen shows you the list of disk drives in your computer, the files in the root directory, and a list of some of the PC DOS programs available.

The IBM DOS Shell can be displayed in different modes and colors. If you have a text-only display, the Shell appears in text mode. If you have a graphics display, the Shell appears in graphics mode

If you have a graphics display, you can show the IBM DOS Shell in graphics mode. In graphics mode, the Shell uses icons to represent disk drives, directories, programs, and text files. Other parts of the display, such as the scroll bars and the mouse pointer, are easier to view in graphics mode.

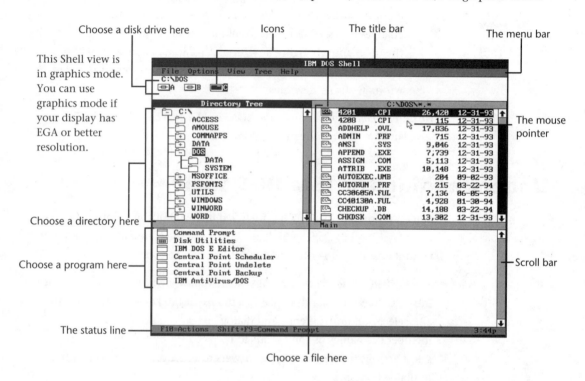

No matter which mode you use to display the IBM DOS Shell, the same basic parts appear on-screen. Table 1.1 describes the basic parts of the Shell display.

1

Table 1.1 IBM DOS Shell Parts

Part	Description
Title bar	Identifies the name of the current window or dialog box.
Menu bar	Provides a list of pull-down menu options. The menu bar is below the title bar of the main window.
Disk drive area	Lists the disk drives your computer recognizes. The selected drive is highlighted.
Directory Tree	Identifies the Directory Tree area. The title area title is highlighted when the area is selected.
Directory Tree area	Shows the directories for the selected drive. The selected directory is highlighted.
Files area title	Identifies the Files area. The title is highlighted when this area is selected.
Files area	Shows the files for the selected directory. The selected file is highlighted.
Program area title	Identifies the program area. The title is highlighted when this area is selected.
Program area	Lists the programs available from the current program group and lists other program groups.
Selection cursor	In text mode, the selection cursor is a small triangular arrow. In graphics mode, it indicates the selected drive, directory, file, or program with a highlighted area or band.
Status line	Shows function key commands, messages, and the current time at the bottom line of the Shell display.
Mouse pointer	Indicates the current position of the mouse on the display.
Scroll bar	Used to view any list of directories, files, or programs that is too long to fit in the display area.

Using the IBM DOS Shell

Remember that to start the IBM DOS Shell from the PC DOS command prompt, you must follow these steps:

1. Type **DOSSHELL**.

2. Press **Enter**.

From the Shell, you can type PC DOS commands, run application programs, find files, view the contents of files, and change the way that the Shell display appears. All these actions are performed by selecting menu options. You do not have to remember command names or the format and parameters of the commands. Just browse through the Shell to see the available commands.

If you decide that you want to enter a command from the standard command line instead of the Shell, you can select Exit from the File menu, press **Alt+F4** (the Exit shortcut key combination), or press the **F3** function key. You can temporarily return to the PC DOS command line by pressing **Shift+F9**. To return to the IBM DOS Shell, type **EXIT** at the PC DOS command prompt.

When you select a menu, the menu commands for that selection drop down.

Choose a menu command here

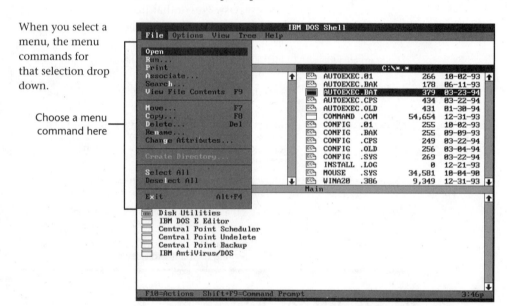

When PC DOS needs you to supply more information to complete a command, PC DOS displays a dialog box. You type the answers to the prompts and choose OK, and PC DOS carries out the command.

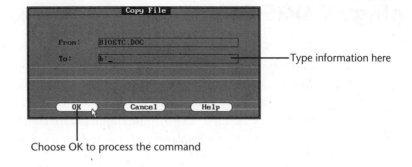

Type information here

Choose OK to process the command

If an item on the Shell screen is highlighted, that item is selected. When one of the disk drive letters is highlighted, that drive is the selected drive, and the list of directories in the Directory Tree area is for the selected drive. When one of the directories in the displayed list is highlighted, this directory is the selected directory, and the list of files in the Files area is for the selected directory. Before you use other Shell commands, you must know which items are selected.

The selected drive

You perform actions and start commands in the Shell by selecting items.

The selected directory

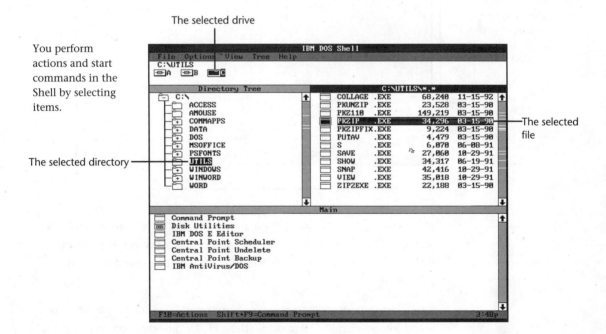

The selected file

Typing PC DOS Commands

To use PC DOS from the PC DOS command prompt, you have to communicate by using the command names that PC DOS understands. PC DOS has more than 100 commands, although you may use only 10 or 12 of them regularly. Most of the command names describe the actions they initiate. For example, COPY is the command for copying a file, and DIR is the command for displaying a list of the contents of a directory.

You type a command into PC DOS to the right of the PC DOS command prompt. Then you press **Enter** to issue the command. PC DOS processes the command and responds accordingly.

Syntax
The precise format you must use when you type a command.

PC DOS is particular about the way you type a command. If you don't get the *syntax* exactly right, PC DOS cannot process the command. If you do not enter spaces in the correct location, for example, PC DOS does not recognize the command.

The PC DOS command prompt   Type the command name here

You must use precise syntax when you type a command in order for PC DOS to respond correctly.

The results of the DIR command

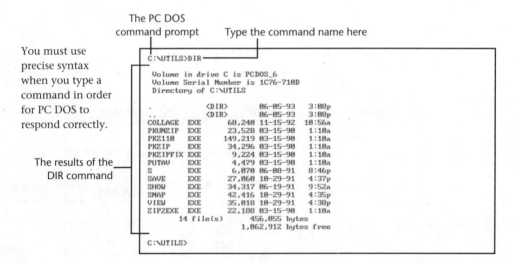

```
C:\UTILS>DIR

 Volume in drive C is PCDOS_6
 Volume Serial Number is 1C76-710D
 Directory of C:\UTILS

 .            <DIR>        06-05-93    3:08p
 ..           <DIR>        06-05-93    3:08p
 COLLAGE  EXE     68,240 11-15-92   10:56a
 PKUNZIP  EXE     23,528 03-15-90    1:10a
 PKZ110   EXE    149,219 03-15-90    1:10a
 PKZIP    EXE     34,296 03-15-90    1:10a
 PKZIPFIX EXE      9,224 03-15-90    1:10a
 PUTAV    EXE      4,479 03-15-90    1:10a
 S        EXE      6,070 06-08-91    8:46p
 SAVE     EXE     27,060 10-29-91    4:37p
 SHOW     EXE     34,317 06-19-91    9:52a
 SNAP     EXE     42,416 10-29-91    4:35p
 VIEW     EXE     35,018 10-29-91    4:38p
 ZIP2EXE  EXE     22,188 03-15-90    1:10a
        14 file(s)       456,055 bytes
                       1,062,912 bytes free

C:\UTILS>
```

If you make a mistake when typing, you can press **Backspace** to delete characters before you press **Enter**. If you press **Enter** before you notice the mistake, you can press **Esc** to try to stop the command before it is carried out.

Case doesn't matter when you type a command; you can type the command in uppercase or lowercase letters. PC DOS reads *COPY*, *copy*, and *Copy* as the same command.

Chapter 2

Making PC DOS Work

On your desk, you now have a complete personal computer system ready for use. You know what all the hardware and software components can do, and you are ready to get to work.

Wouldn't you like to be able to just sit down in front of your computer and say, "Start up, and load Word for Windows so that I can create a document in a directory called Winword Docs," and have the computer respond? But you can't. That's why you need PC DOS.

In this chapter, you learn to use PC DOS to put your computer to work. You learn to use basic commands to manage disks, files, and directories.

Note: *Many of the commands used in this chapter are covered in more detail in Appendix A, "The PC DOS Top Twenty."*

Starting PC DOS

Cold Boot
To turn on your computer by using the power switch.

PC DOS starts automatically when you start, or boot, your computer. If your computer is off, you start it by using a *cold boot*. To cold boot your computer, press the On/Off switch into the On position. Look for the On/Off switch on the front of your computer. Your display probably has a separate On/Off switch; if so, you must turn this switch to On as well.

As soon as you turn on your computer, it begins running a Power-On Self Test (POST) to make sure that all components are working properly. You will probably hear sounds and see information on-screen as the system starts. Some computers count the available memory during the POST and display the amount in a message on-screen, as in the following:

```
003712 KB
OK Wait
```

If you have problems...

If you see the following message, your computer cannot find PC DOS.

```
Non-system disk or disk error
Replace and strike any key when ready
```

If PC DOS is installed on the hard disk, make sure that drive A does not have a diskette inserted in it. Press any key to try loading PC DOS again. You must install PC DOS before you can use your computer.

When the POST is complete, PC DOS starts. It carries out the commands in the CONFIG.SYS file, and then it carries out the commands in the AUTOEXEC.BAT file. (For more information on CONFIG.SYS and AUTOEXEC.BAT, see Chapter 1, "Understanding System Basics," and Chapter 8, "Configuring Your Personal Computer.") As PC DOS starts, you will probably see an on-screen message similar to the following one, indicating that PC DOS is loading into memory, as well as other messages as PC DOS carries out the commands in the CONFIG.SYS and AUTOEXEC.BAT files.

```
Starting PC DOS...

Microsoft (R) Mouse Driver Version 8.20
Copyright (C) Microsoft Corp. 1983-1992.
Copyright (C) IBM Corp. 1992-1993
Mouse driver installed.
```

On some systems, PC DOS may prompt you to enter the date and time during start-up. To enter the date, follow these steps:

1. Type the current date, using the format indicated within the parentheses on the command line.

2. Press **Enter**.

When PC DOS prompts you for the date, it also prompts for the time. To enter the time, follow these steps:

1. Type the current time, using the format indicated within the parentheses on the command line.

2. Press **Enter**.

Note: *For more information on setting the date and time, see the section "Setting the Date and Time," later in this chapter.*

When you have successfully loaded PC DOS, the following PC DOS command prompt appears on-screen:

```
c:\>
```

Usually, the PC DOS command prompt displays the current drive (C:), the current directory (\), and the prompt symbol >, but the prompt can appear differently on your computer. For information on changing the appearance of the PC DOS command prompt, see the section "Changing the PC DOS Command Prompt," later in this chapter.

If you have problems...

If someone added a command to your AUTOEXEC.BAT file to display something other than the PC DOS command prompt, you may see something different on-screen when PC DOS starts. For example, your computer may display the IBM DOS Shell, or Windows, or a customized menu screen. For information on what to do when your computer displays the IBM DOS Shell, see Chapter 1, "Understanding System Basics." For information on what to do when your computer displays Windows, see Chapter 3, "Working with the Windows Desktop." For information on what to do if your computer displays a customized menu, consult the documentation that came with the application program, or contact your company's support staff.

Restarting PC DOS

Warm boot
The restarting of your computer without turning off the power.

When necessary, you can use a *warm boot* to restart PC DOS without turning your computer off and then on again. A warm boot is faster than a cold boot and saves wear and tear on your hardware.

Caution
Restart PC DOS
only if your system
will not respond to
commands. Restart-
ing PC DOS with-
out exiting all
application pro-
grams can damage
files and data.

To perform a warm boot, follow these steps:

1. Press and hold down **Ctrl**.

2. While still holding down **Ctrl**, press and hold down **Alt**.

3. While still holding down **Ctrl** and **Alt**, press and hold down **Del**.

4. Release all three keys at the same time. The computer skips the POST and immediately loads PC DOS.

**If you have
problems...**

If nothing happens when you release the keys, try pressing and releasing **Ctrl+Alt+Del** again. If nothing happens, turn off your computer. Wait a minute or so before you turn it on again.

Some computers also have a Reset button. Pressing the Reset button is the same as performing a warm boot.

Turning Off Your Computer

You should turn off the computer only when you are at a PC DOS command prompt and you have already closed all other application programs, including Windows. When you are working in an application program, save all files and exit the program before you turn off the computer.

To turn off your computer, follow these steps:

1. Locate the power switch on your computer.

2. Gently press the power switch into the Off position.

3. When necessary, turn off your display as well.

Changing the PC DOS Command Prompt

By default, the PC DOS command prompt displays the current drive, directory, and the prompt symbol >. You can modify the appearance of the prompt by using the PROMPT command.

To change the appearance of the prompt to include the current date, follow these steps:

1. Type **PROMPT**.

2. Press the **spacebar** once to insert a space between the PROMPT command and the description of the type of prompt you want.

3. Type **PD$G**. This identifies a prompt that includes the current directory.

4. Press **Enter**. PC DOS changes the prompt to include the current directory, which should look like the following:

   ```
   C:\Wed 05-18-1995>
   ```

This prompt includes the symbols for the current drive (C:), the current directory (\), the current date (Wed 05-18-1995), and the prompt symbol (>).

Getting Help

Whenever you are working with PC DOS, you can use the HELP command to display Help about any command. Help is useful when you forget which command you should use to accomplish a specific task or when you need additional information about how to type a command correctly.

To display a list of all PC DOS commands, follow these steps:

1. At the PC DOS command prompt, type **HELP**.

2. Press **Enter**. PC DOS displays an alphabetical list of PC DOS commands on-screen, along with brief descriptions of what each command does.

3. Press any key to display the next screen of commands.

Type the HELP command at the PC
DOS command prompt

Use the HELP
command to
display informa-
tion about PC DOS
commands.

The list of PC DOS
commands

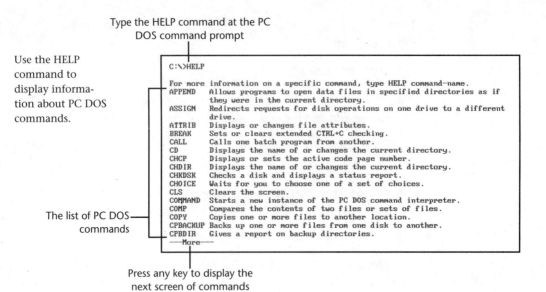

```
C:\>HELP

For more information on a specific command, type HELP command-name.
APPEND    Allows programs to open data files in specified directories as if
          they were in the current directory.
ASSIGN    Redirects requests for disk operations on one drive to a different
          drive.
ATTRIB    Displays or changes file attributes.
BREAK     Sets or clears extended CTRL+C checking.
CALL      Calls one batch program from another.
CD        Displays the name of or changes the current directory.
CHCP      Displays or sets the active code page number.
CHDIR     Displays the name of or changes the current directory.
CHKDSK    Checks a disk and displays a status report.
CHOICE    Waits for you to choose one of a set of choices.
CLS       Clears the screen.
COMMAND   Starts a new instance of the PC DOS command interpreter.
COMP      Compares the contents of two files or sets of files.
COPY      Copies one or more files to another location.
CPBACKUP  Backs up one or more files from one disk to another.
CPBDIR    Gives a report on backup directories.
---More---
```

Press any key to display the
next screen of commands

When you know the command name, but you need more information about how to type it correctly, you can use the HELP command to display detailed information about the command.

To display information about a particular PC DOS command, follow these steps:

1. At the PC DOS command prompt, type **HELP**.

2. Press the **spacebar** once to leave a space between the HELP command and the name of the command about which you need information.

3. Type the name of the command about which you need information, as in the following:

   ```
   C:\>HELP PROMPT
   ```

4. Press **Enter**. PC DOS displays information about how to use the specified command.

PC DOS displays
information about
the proper way to
use the PROMPT
command.

```
Changes the PC DOS command prompt.

PROMPT [text]

    text    Specifies a new command prompt.

Prompt can be made up of normal characters and the following special codes:

    $Q    = (equal sign)
    $$    $ (dollar sign)
    $T    Current time
    $D    Current date
    $P    Current drive and path
    $V    PC DOS version number
    $N    Current drive
    $G    > (greater-than sign)
    $L    < (less-than sign)
    $B    | (pipe)
    $H    Backspace (erases previous character)
    $E    Escape code (ASCII code 27)
    $_    Carriage return and linefeed

Type PROMPT without parameters to reset the prompt to the default setting.

C:\>
```

Making a Directory

By using directories, you and PC DOS can keep your files organized. The logical way PC DOS arranges directories and files on a disk always enables you to locate the files you need. (For information about how PC DOS organizes stored data, see Chapter 1, "Understanding System Basics.")

To make a directory, follow these steps:

1. At the PC DOS command prompt, type **MD**, the command for making a directory.

2. Type the path, followed by the name of the directory you want PC DOS to make, as in the following:

       C:\>MD\DATA

   The C:\> is the PC DOS command prompt, the MD is the Make Directory command, the \ is the current directory, and DATA is the new directory name—a subdirectory of the root directory.

3. Press **Enter**. PC DOS makes the directory.

If you have problems...

When you cannot find the directory you just made, you may have typed the wrong path.

When you do not type the entire path to the new directory, PC DOS makes the directory a subdirectory of the current directory.

Changing Directories

**Current
directory**
The directory PC
DOS is currently
working in.

Unless you specify otherwise, PC DOS carries out commands on the
current directory.

You can specify a directory every time you type a command, or you can
change to the directory you want to make current. The command to
change the current directory is a useful one because you can use it to
navigate around the directory structure by moving from directory to
directory.

To change directories, follow these steps:

1. At the PC DOS command prompt, type **CD**, the command for
    changing the current directory.

2. Type the path to the directory you want to make current.

3. Press **Enter**. PC DOS makes the specified directory the current
    directory. When your prompt is set to display the current directory,
    you see the directory name in the prompt:

    ```
    C:\>CD\DATA
    C:\DATA>
    ```

    The PC DOS command prompt indicates that \DATA is now the
    current directory.

**If you have
problems...**

When you see the message Invalid directory, check your typing to
make sure that you have spelled the directory name correctly. You may have
tried to change to a directory that does not exist. You must create the directory before you can change to it. See the section "Making a Directory,"
earlier in this chapter.

If you are in the current directory and you want to maintain files and
disks, issue commands, and start application programs in that directory,
you do not have to specify a directory path each time you type the
command.

Note: *To change to the root directory from any other directory, type **CD** and
then press **Enter**.*

Removing a Directory

It is important to keep your disk free of old and unused files and directories. Unused directories take up valuable disk space. When you accidentally make a directory or have an old directory you no longer need, you can remove it from your disk.

Note: *You can use the RD (remove directory) command only to remove an empty directory. If the directory contains files or subdirectories that you want to remove, you must delete them first, or use the DELTREE command. Use the RD command to delete subdirectories. Use the DEL command to delete files. For information on deleting files, see the section "Deleting Files," later in this chapter.*

To remove a directory, follow these steps:

1. Change to the directory that contains the directory you want to remove.

2. Type **RD**, the command for removing a directory, followed by the path and the name of the directory you want to remove.

        C:\>RD DATA

3. Press **Enter**. PC DOS removes the directory.

If you have problems...

When you see the message Invalid path, not directory, or directory not empty, you have mistyped the path or directory name, or there are still files or subdirectories in the directory.

Displaying the Contents of a Directory

You can use PC DOS to display a list of files and directories contained on any disk or in any directory.

To display a list of all files and directories in the current directory, follow these steps:

1. Change to the directory you want to make current.

2. At the PC DOS command prompt, type **DIR**, the command for displaying files and directories.

3. Press **Enter**. PC DOS displays a list of the files and directories in the current directory.

Notice that the following information appears on-screen:

Information Provided in Column	Description
File name	The root of the file name (up to eight characters) appears first.
Extension	The extension is listed in the second column.
Directory	When the entry is a directory, you see <DIR> in the third column.
File Size	The fourth column lists the size of the file. The size is measured in bytes. One byte equals about one character. When the entry is a directory, nothing is listed.
Date	The fifth column displays the date when the file was created or modified.
Time	The final column displays the time when the file was created or modified.

The two lines at the end of the directory listing display the number of files, bytes used, and bytes free (disk space remaining). The PC DOS command prompt appears at the bottom of the listing so that you can type the next command.

The DIR command displays the files and directories contained in a directory.

The DIR command

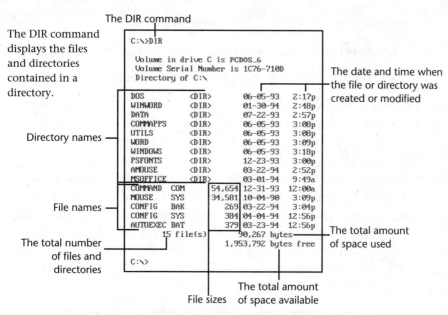

```
C:\>DIR

    Volume in drive C is PCDOS_6
    Volume Serial Number is 1C76-710D
    Directory of C:\

    DOS          <DIR>          06-05-93    2:17p
    WINWORD      <DIR>          01-30-94    2:48p
    DATA         <DIR>          07-22-93    2:57p
    COMMAPPS     <DIR>          06-05-93    3:08p
    UTILS        <DIR>          06-05-93    3:08p
    WORD         <DIR>          06-05-93    3:09p
    WINDOWS      <DIR>          06-05-93    3:18p
    PSFONTS      <DIR>          12-23-93    3:00p
    AMOUSE       <DIR>          03-22-94    2:52p
    MSOFFICE     <DIR>          03-01-94    9:49a
    COMMAND  COM    54,654      12-31-93   12:00a
    MOUSE    SYS    34,581      10-04-90    3:09p
    CONFIG   BAK       269      03-22-94    3:04p
    CONFIG   SYS       384      04-04-94   12:56p
    AUTOEXEC BAT       379      03-23-94   12:56p
            15 file(s)       90,267 bytes
                          1,953,792 bytes free

    C:\>
```

Directory names

File names

The total number of files and directories

The date and time when the file or directory was created or modified

The total amount of space used

File sizes   The total amount of space available

Modifying a Directory List

Switch

Turns on an optional function of a command.

Parameter

Any additional information you type after the command name to refine what you want the command to do.

You can modify the way PC DOS lists the contents of a directory on-screen by adding *switches* and *parameters* to the DIR command.

Changing the appearance of the listing is useful when you have too many files to display on one screen, when you need to display only certain files, or when you want to display only certain information about the files. (For more information about using the DIR command, consult Appendix A, "The PC DOS Top Twenty.")

Displaying a Wide File Listing

When you want to see more of the contents of a large disk or directory on-screen at one time, you can add a switch to the DIR command to tell PC DOS to display a wide file listing.

A wide file listing shows multiple columns of file and directory names. It does not display any additional information.

To display a wide file listing, follow these steps:

1. At the PC DOS command prompt, type **DIR**.

2. Type **/W**, the switch that tells PC DOS to display a wide file listing. (The W can be uppercase or lowercase.)

3. Press **Enter**. PC DOS displays a wide file listing of the current directory.

Notice that only file and directory names are listed in five columns across the screen. The other file information (size, date, and time) does not appear. Directories appear in brackets, and the last two lines of the listing display the number of files, number of bytes used, and number of bytes free.

Type the command and the
command switch here

Directory names are
enclosed in brackets

In a wide file
listing, only the
file or directory
name is displayed.

```
C:\>DIR /W

    Volume in drive C is PCDOS_6
    Volume Serial Number is 1C76-710D
    Directory of C:\

[DOS]           [WINWORD]       [DATA]          [COMMAPPS]      [UTILS]
[WORD]          [WINDOWS]       [PSFONTS]       [AMOUSE]        [MSOFFICE]
COMMAND.COM     WINA20.386      MOUSE.SYS       CONFIG.CPS      [ACCESS]
AUTOEXEC.CPS    CONFIG.SYS      AUTOEXEC.BAT
         18 file(s)         99,915 bytes
                           991,232 bytes free

C:\>
```

File names have
extensions

Displaying a Directory List One Page at a Time

When the directory contains many files and directories, you can tell PC DOS to display only one page at a time. PC DOS pauses until you tell it to display the next page, giving you a chance to read the list.

To display a directory list one page at a time, follow these steps:

1. Change to the directory you want to list.

2. At the PC DOS command prompt, type **DIR**.

3. Type **/P**, the switch that tells PC DOS to pause between pages in a directory listing.

4. Press **Enter**. PC DOS displays the first page of files.

5. Press any key when you are ready to display the next page.

When you use the /P switch with the DIR command, PC DOS pauses at the bottom of the page until you press any key to continue.

```
Volume in drive C is PCDOS_6
Volume Serial Number is 1C76-710D
Directory of C:\

TEST           <DIR>          03-26-94   12:53p
DOS            <DIR>          06-05-93    2:17p
WINWORD        <DIR>          01-30-94    2:48p
DATA           <DIR>          07-22-93    2:57p
COMMAPPS       <DIR>          06-05-93    3:08p
UTILS          <DIR>          06-05-93    3:08p
WORD           <DIR>          06-05-93    3:09p
WINDOWS        <DIR>          06-05-93    3:18p
PSFONTS        <DIR>          12-23-93    3:00p
AMOUSE         <DIR>          03-22-94    2:52p
MSOFFICE       <DIR>          03-01-94    9:49a
COMMAND  COM      54,654   12-31-93   12:00a
WINA20   386       9,349   12-31-93   12:00a
MOUSE    SYS      34,581   10-04-90    3:09p
CONFIG   CPS         249   03-22-94    2:28p
ACCESS         <DIR>          03-01-94   10:32a
AUTOEXEC CPS         434   03-22-94    2:59p
CONFIG   SYS         269   03-22-94    3:04p
AUTOEXEC BAT         379   03-23-94   12:56p
Press any key to continue . . .
```

Listing Selected Files

You can use PC DOS wild card characters to display only selected files in a directory listing. For information about wild card characters, see Chapter 1, "Understanding System Basics."

To display only selected files, follow these steps:

1. Change to the directory you want to make current.

2. At the PC DOS command prompt, type **DIR**.

3. Press the **spacebar** once to leave a space between the command name and the parameter you are about to type.

4. Specify the files you want to list by using wild card characters as follows:

■ Use * in place of any one character, and any character that follows it. For example, type ***.DOC** to list all files with the extension DOC.

■ Use ? in place of any one character. For example, type **?FILE.DOC** to list files that begin with any character, followed by FILE.DOC. This would include 1FILE.DOC, 2FILE.DOC, and so on—but not 10FILE.DOC. (Type **??FILE.DOC** to get 10 FILE.DOC.)

5. Press **Enter**. PC DOS displays a list of all files that match the file specification you entered on the command line.

Type the file specifications

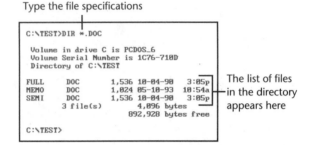

PC DOS lists all files in the \TEST directory that match the file specification *.DOC

The list of files in the directory appears here

Listing Directories in a Tree Diagram

You can display a tree diagram of directories and subdirectories by using the TREE command.

To display a tree diagram of directories, follow these steps:

1. Change to the directory you want to make current.

2. At the PC DOS command prompt, type **TREE**.

3. Press **Enter**. PC DOS displays a tree diagram of all directories in the current directory, and their subdirectories.

Type the TREE command

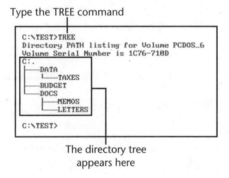

By using the TREE command, you can see on-screen the relationship between directories.

The directory tree appears here

Clearing the Screen

Sometimes the PC DOS screen can become cluttered with information. You can use the CLS (clear screen) command to clear all information from the screen except the PC DOS command prompt.

To clear the screen, follow these steps:

1. At the PC DOS command prompt, type **CLS**.

2. Press **Enter**. PC DOS displays the PC DOS command prompt at the top of an empty screen.

Inserting Diskettes

To transfer data into and to take the data from your computer, you can use diskettes. When handling diskettes, you must be careful not to damage them. (For information about diskettes and disk types, see Chapter 1, "Understanding System Basics.")

To insert a diskette into a diskette drive, follow these steps:

1. Hold the diskette so that the label is facing up.

If you have problems...   If you are using a 5 1/4-inch diskette that doesn't have a label, hold the diskette so that the notched side is on the left. If you are using a 3 1/2-inch diskette that does not have a label, look for writing (diskette type, arrow, manufacturer, for example) to indicate the side that should face up. Hold the diskette so that you see the writing.

---

2. Gently insert the diskette into the drive, and then take one of the following actions:

- When you are using a 5 1/4-inch diskette, you must shut the drive door. Push the lever so that it is closed.

- When you are using a 3 1/2-inch diskette, you should hear a click, indicating that the diskette is inserted. The eject button pops out.

Changing the Current Drive

Current Drive
The drive in
which PC DOS
is working.

Unless otherwise specified, PC DOS carries out all commands on the *current drive*.

You can change the current drive so that you do not have to specify a different drive every time you type a command.

To change the current drive, follow these steps:

1. Insert a diskette into the drive you want to make current.

2. At the PC DOS command prompt, type the letter of the drive you want to make current.

3. Immediately to the right of the drive letter, type a colon (:).
   For drive A, the command line should look like the following:

   ```
   C:\>A:
   ```

4. Press **Enter**.

5. PC DOS makes the specified drive the current drive. The PC DOS command prompt changes to show the current drive.

   ```
   A:\>
   ```

**If you have
problems...**

If you see an error message similar to the following, you have not inserted a diskette into the drive you want to make current or you inserted an unformatted diskette.

```
Not ready reading drive A
Abort, Retry, Fail?
```

Insert a diskette and press **R** to try again.

Formatting a Diskette

Before you can store information on a diskette, it must be formatted. Formatting prepares the diskette so that PC DOS can write information on it and then find the information when it is needed.

Note: *Formatting erases all information on a diskette. Make sure that the diskette you are formatting is blank or that you do not need the existing files.*

To format a diskette, follow these steps:

1. Insert a blank diskette into the drive, either A or B, you want to use. To see whether anything is on the diskette, use the DIR command.

2. At the PC DOS command prompt, type **FORMAT**.

Caution
Do not use the FORMAT command on your hard disk. Formatting erases all data on the disk.

3. Press the **spacebar** once.

4. Type the letter of the drive you are using and then type a colon.

5. Press **Enter**.

6. PC DOS prompts you to insert a new diskette into the specified drive, even when you have already done so.

7. Make sure that the diskette you want to format is correctly inserted in the drive, and then press **Enter**.

FORMAT checks the existing disk format. If that format differs from the one being requested, FORMAT prompts you to confirm the procedure.

Volume Label
A name for a diskette.

8. When the format is complete, PC DOS prompts you to enter a *volume label*. If the prompt appears, type the label and press **Enter** or just press **Enter** if you don't want to have a volume label.

9. PC DOS displays information about the diskette just formatted and then asks whether you want to format another. Press **Y** to format another diskette. Press **N** to return to the PC DOS command prompt.

Type the FORMAT command here

Formatting erases
all existing data on
the diskette. Make
sure that the
diskette is blank or
that you do not
need the data
anymore.

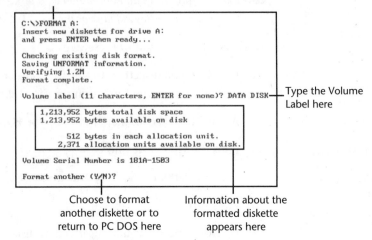

Type the Volume
Label here

Choose to format
another diskette or to
return to PC DOS here

Information about the
formatted diskette
appears here

Changing a Volume Label

You can change a volume label any time after a diskette has been
formatted without affecting the data stored on the diskette.

To view the current volume label, follow these steps:

1. If necessary, insert the diskette into the diskette drive.

2. Make the drive that contains the diskette the current drive.

3. At the PC DOS command prompt, type **VOL**.

4. Press **Enter**. PC DOS displays the volume label and the volume
   serial number.

Use the VOL
command to
display the label of
the diskette in the
current drive.

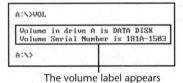

The volume label appears

To change the volume label, follow these steps:

1. If necessary, insert the diskette into the diskette drive.

2. Make the drive that contains the diskette the current drive.

3. At the PC DOS command prompt, type **LABEL**.

4. Press **Enter**. PC DOS displays the current volume label and the volume serial number and prompts you to enter a new label.

Use the LABEL command to change the label of the diskette in the current drive.

Type the VOL command here

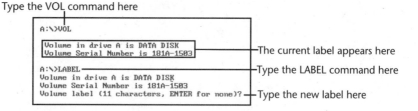

```
A:\>VOL

  ┌─────────────────────────────────────┐
  │ Volume in drive A is DATA DISK       │
  │ Volume Serial Number is 181A-1503    │
  └─────────────────────────────────────┘── The current label appears here
A:\>LABEL ──────────────────────────────────── Type the LABEL command here
Volume in drive A is DATA DISK
Volume Serial Number is 181A-1503
Volume label (11 characters, ENTER for none)? ── Type the new label here
```

5. Type the new label.

6. Press **Enter**. PC DOS changes the label. Use the VOL command to view the new label name.

Copying a Diskette

You can copy the entire contents of one diskette to another diskette of the same size and capacity by using the DISKCOPY command. (For information about diskette sizes and capacities, see Chapter 1, "Understanding System Basics.")

Copying diskettes is easier when you have two diskette drives of the same size, but you can copy a diskette using one drive as well.

Note: *DISKCOPY copies everything from the old diskette to the new diskette. If the diskette you are copying has errors, the errors will be copied to the new diskette as well.*

Copying a Diskette Using Two Diskette Drives

In order to copy a diskette using two diskette drives, the drives must be the same size. Therefore, you must have two 5 1/4-inch drives or two 3 1/2-inch drives.

Source diskette
The diskette that contains the information you want to copy.

To copy a diskette using two diskette drives of equal size, follow these steps:

1. Insert the *source diskette* into drive A.

Target diskette
The diskette to which you want to copy the information.

2. Insert the *target diskette* into drive B.

3. At the PC DOS command prompt, type **DISKCOPY**.

4. Press the **spacebar** once.

5. Type **A:**.

6. Press the **spacebar** once.

7. Type **B:**.

8. Press **Enter**.

9. PC DOS prompts you to insert the source and target diskettes into the correct drives, even when you have already done so.

Type the DISKCOPY command here

You can easily copy from one diskette to another using two diskette drives of equal size.

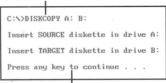

```
C:\>DISKCOPY A: B:
Insert SOURCE diskette in drive A:
Insert TARGET diskette in drive B:
Press any key to continue . . .
```

Press any key to begin the copy process

10. Press any key to continue. PC DOS begins copying the diskette.

11. When PC DOS finishes copying the diskette, it asks whether you want to copy another one. If you want to copy another diskette, press **Y** and then **Enter**. If you want to return to the PC DOS command prompt, press **N** and then **Enter**.

If you have problems...

If you see the following message, you tried to use two drives or two diskettes that are not the same size or capacity.

```
Drive types or diskette types not compatible
Copy process ended
```

Use the procedure described in the next section to copy a diskette using only one drive.

Copying a Diskette Using One Diskette Drive

Even if you have only one diskette drive or two diskette drives of different sizes, you can use the DISKCOPY command to copy a diskette.

To copy a diskette using a single diskette drive, follow these steps:

1. Insert the source diskette into drive A.

2. At the PC DOS command prompt, type **DISKCOPY**.

3. Press the **spacebar** once.

4. Type **A:**.

5. Press the **spacebar** once.

6. Type **A:**.

7. Press **Enter**. PC DOS prompts you to insert the source diskette into drive A.

8. Press any key to begin the copy process.

9. PC DOS prompts you to insert the target diskette into drive A. Remove the source diskette, and insert the target diskette.

   PC DOS prompts you each time you need to swap the diskettes in drive A. Depending on how many bytes the diskette holds and the amount of memory on your computer, you may have to swap diskettes several times.

10. When the diskette has been completely copied, PC DOS asks whether you want to copy another one. If you want to copy another diskette, press **Y** and then **Enter**. If you want to return to the PC DOS command prompt, press **N** and then **Enter**.

Displaying the Contents of a File

You can view the contents of a file without affecting the file by using the TYPE command.

To display the contents of a file, follow these steps:

1. Change to the directory that contains the file you want to display.

2. At the PC DOS command prompt, type the word **TYPE**.

3. Press the **spacebar** once.

4. Type the name of the file that you want to display.

5. Press **Enter**. PC DOS displays the contents of the file on-screen.

Type the command here

PC DOS displays
the contents of the
AUTOEXEC.BAT
file.

The contents of
the file appear here

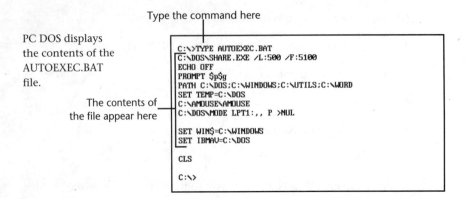

```
C:\>TYPE AUTOEXEC.BAT
C:\DOS\SHARE.EXE /L:500 /F:5100
ECHO OFF
PROMPT $p$g
PATH C:\DOS;C:\WINDOWS;C:\UTILS;C:\WORD
SET TEMP=C:\DOS
C:\AMOUSE\AMOUSE
C:\DOS\MODE LPT1:,, P >NUL

SET WINS=C:\WINDOWS
SET IBMAV=C:\DOS

CLS

C:\>
```

For information on editing a file, see Chapter 7, "Working with the Text Editor."

Copying a File

With PC DOS, you can quickly make copies of existing files. You can copy a file to the same directory, from one directory to another, or from one disk to another. You can even copy groups of files at the same time.

Note: *When you copy a file to a disk, you can take it to another computer, or you can keep it in a safe place to use as a backup.*

Copying a File to the Same Directory

To copy a file to the same directory, follow these steps:

1. Change to the directory that contains the file you want to copy.

2. At the PC DOS command prompt, type **COPY**.

3. Press the **spacebar** once.

4. Type the name of the file you want to copy.

5. Press the **spacebar** once.

6. Type the name you want to assign to the copy of the file. The command should look like the following:

```
C:\>COPY AUTOEXEC.BAT AUTOEXEC.OLD
```

7. Press **Enter**. PC DOS copies the file and displays the message

```
1 file(s) copied
```

Now there are two copies of the same file in the current directory. One copy is named AUTOEXEC.BAT, and one is named AUTOEXEC.OLD. You have two versions of the same file, but they have different names.

Copying a File to a Different Directory or Drive

To copy a file to a different directory or drive, follow these steps:

1. Change to the directory that contains the file you want to copy.

2. At the PC DOS command prompt, type **COPY**.

3. Press the **spacebar** once.

4. Type the name of the file you want to copy.

5. Press the **spacebar** once.

6. Type the path to the location where you want to store the copy. Include a drive letter, if necessary. The command should look like the following:

```
C:\>COPY AUTOEXEC.BAT C:\TEST\DATA
```

Because you are using the same file name, you do not have to type it after the new location name.

7. Press **Enter**. PC DOS copies the file and displays the message

```
1 file(s) copied
```

The original AUTOEXEC.BAT file is still in the root directory, and a copy of the AUTOEXEC.BAT file is in the C:\TEST\DATA subdirectory.

Copy a Group of Files to Another Location

To copy a group of files to another drive or directory, follow these steps:

1. Change to the directory that contains the files you want to copy.

2. At the PC DOS command prompt, type **COPY**.

3. Press the **spacebar** once.

4. Using wild card characters, type the file specification for the group of files you want to copy. For example, type ***.DOC** to copy all files with the extension DOC, or type ***.*** to copy all files.

5. Press the **spacebar** once.

6. Type the path to the location where you want to store the copied files.

7. Press **Enter**. PC DOS copies all the files that match the file specification to the new location and displays the name of each file as it is copied.

Type the COPY command here

All the files with the extension DOC have been copied from the \TEST directory to a diskette in drive A.

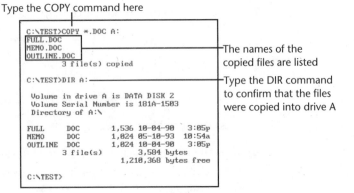

```
C:\TEST>COPY *.DOC A:
FULL.DOC
MEMO.DOC
OUTLINE.DOC
          3 file(s) copied

C:\TEST>DIR A:

   Volume in drive A is DATA DISK 2
   Volume Serial Number is 181A-1503
   Directory of A:\

FULL      DOC      1,536 10-04-90    3:05p
MEMO      DOC      1,024 05-10-93   10:54a
OUTLINE   DOC      1,024 10-04-90    3:05p
          3 file(s)         3,584 bytes
                        1,210,368 bytes free

C:\TEST>
```

The names of the copied files are listed

Type the DIR command to confirm that the files were copied into drive A

Renaming a File

You can use PC DOS to rename an existing file, without affecting the contents of the file.

To rename a file, follow these steps:

1. Change to the directory that contains the file you want to rename.

2. At the PC DOS command prompt, type **RENAME**.

3. Press the **spacebar** once.

4. Type the current name of the file you want to rename. To rename a group of files, use the wild-card characters.

5. Press the **spacebar** once.

6. Type the new name you want to give to the file.

7. Press **Enter**. PC DOS renames the file.

Deleting Files

When you no longer need a file, you can delete it so that it doesn't take up valuable disk space. You can delete one file, or you can use wild card characters to specify a group of files to delete.

Note: *Before you delete a file, you should make sure that the file does not contain data that you need.*

To delete a file, follow these steps:

1. Change to the directory that contains the file you want to delete.

2. At the PC DOS command prompt, type **DEL**.

3. Press the **spacebar** once.

4. Type the name of the file you want to delete. To delete a group of files, type the file specification, using wild card characters.

5. Press **Enter**. PC DOS deletes the specified file.

If you have problems...   When you delete a file by accident, you may be able to recover it by using the Undelete utility. For more information on undeleting files, see Chapter 10, "Using IBM Tools."

Checking the Condition of a Disk

With PC DOS, you can find out how much space is available on a disk, as well as whether the disk is in good condition.

To check a disk, follow these steps:

1. At the PC DOS command prompt, type **CHKDSK**.

2. Press **Enter**. PC DOS checks the disk and displays a status report about the disk's condition and available memory.

The CHKDSK status report displays information in three sections:

■ The first section displays information about the number, size, and condition of files as well as the directories on the disk.

■ The middle section displays information about how much disk space has been allocated, or used, by the files and directories.

■ The third section displays information about system memory.

Type the command here

By using CHKDSK, you can quickly determine the status and condition of your disks. The disk being checked in this report is in good condition.

```
C:\>CHKDSK

Volume PCDOS_6     created 03-27-1994 11:23a
Volume Serial Number is 1C76-710D

    85,018,624 bytes total disk space
    12,652,544 bytes in 5 hidden files
       149,504 bytes in 60 directories
    71,479,296 bytes in 1,420 user files
       737,280 bytes available on disk

         2,048 bytes in each allocation unit
        41,513 total allocation units on disk
           360 available allocation units on disk

       655,360 total bytes memory
       528,464 bytes free

C:\>
```

File and directory information appears here

Allocation information appears here

System memory information appears here

When CHKDSK finds allocation errors, a message appears at the top of the status report. You can fix these errors by using the /F switch with the CHKDSK command. Just type **CHKDSK /F** and press **Enter**. Then PC DOS fixes the error.

This diskette has allocation errors that can be fixed using the CHKDSK command.

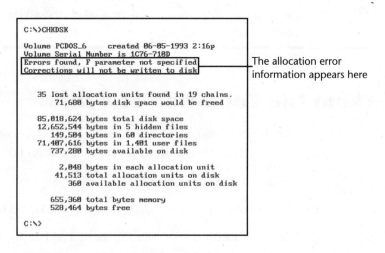

```
C:\>CHKDSK

Volume PCDOS_6     created 06-05-1993 2:16p
Volume Serial Number is 1C76-710D
Errors found, F parameter not specified
Corrections will not be written to disk

    35 lost allocation units found in 19 chains.
       71,680 bytes disk space would be freed

    85,018,624 bytes total disk space
    12,652,544 bytes in 5 hidden files
       149,504 bytes in 60 directories
    71,407,616 bytes in 1,401 user files
       737,280 bytes available on disk

         2,048 bytes in each allocation unit
        41,513 total allocation units on disk
           360 available allocation units on disk

       655,360 total bytes memory
       528,464 bytes free

C:\>
```

The allocation error information appears here

When CHKDSK finds bad sectors on the disk, you should not use the disk. Bad sectors are areas of the disk where data cannot be written to or read from correctly by the computer. You may be able to copy files from the good sectors on the disk to another disk by using the COPY command. For more information, see the section "Copying a File," earlier in this chapter.

This diskette has bad sectors and should be thrown away.

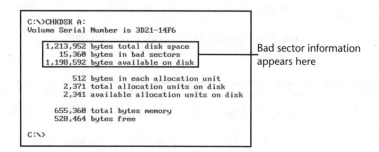

```
C:\>CHKDSK A:
Volume Serial Number is 3D21-14F6

    1,213,952 bytes total disk space
       15,360 bytes in bad sectors
    1,198,592 bytes available on disk

          512 bytes in each allocation unit
        2,371 total allocation units on disk
        2,341 available allocation units on disk

      655,360 total bytes memory
      528,464 bytes free

C:\>
```

Bad sector information appears here

Setting the Date and Time

Personal computers have clocks and calendars that they use to keep track of the time that a file is saved to disk. When you use DIR to list the contents of a directory, you see the date and time on-screen. Some application programs display the time on-screen as you work.

Most computers are set to automatically keep track of the date and time, but some ask you to enter the date and time each time you start the computer. For more information, see the section "Starting PC DOS," earlier in this chapter.

You can change the date and time whenever you want, which is useful for keeping up with daylight savings time or leap year—or when you move your computer across time zones.

To change the date, follow these steps:

1. At the PC DOS command prompt, type **DATE**.

2. Press **Enter**. PC DOS displays the current date and prompts you to enter a new date.

You can check the
system date or
enter a new date
by using the DATE
command.

Type the command here

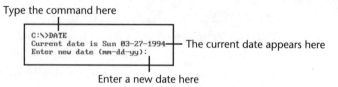

```
C:\>DATE
Current date is Sun 03-27-1994
Enter new date (mm-dd-yy):
```

The current date appears here

Enter a new date here

3. Type the date using the format shown within the parentheses on the command line: mm-dd-yy.

4. Press **Enter**. PC DOS changes the date.

If you have problems...

If you have already issued the DATE command but decide that you do not want to change the date, press **Enter** without typing a new date.

If you typed the wrong date, repeat the preceding steps.

To change the time, follow these steps:

1. At the PC DOS command prompt, type **TIME**.

2. Press **Enter**. PC DOS displays the current time and prompts you to enter a new time.

You can check the
system time or
enter a new time
by using the TIME
command.

Type the command here

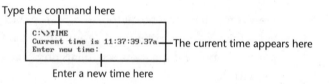

```
C:\>TIME
Current time is 11:37:39.37a
Enter new time:
```

The current time appears here

Enter a new time here

3. Type the time, using the format that PC DOS uses to display the current time: hh:mm:ssa (for a.m.) or hh:mm:ssp (for p.m.). You do not have to enter seconds.

4. Press **Enter**. PC DOS changes the time.

If you have problems...

If you have already issued the TIME command but decide that you do not want to change the time, press **Enter** without typing a new time.

Setting the Path

PC DOS looks for application programs and commands in the current directory on the current disk. When you want PC DOS to carry out a command or start an application program that is stored somewhere other than in the current directory or disk, you can choose one of three actions:

■ You can change directories or disks before you type the command.

■ You can type the path to the different location on the command line each time you type a command.

■ You can use the PATH command to set PC DOS to look for commands in another directory or disk.

Note: *You can include the PATH command in your AUTOEXEC.BAT file so that each time you start your computer PC DOS automatically looks in certain directories for application programs and commands. PATH commands entered at the PC DOS command line take precedence over PATH commands in the AUTOEXEC.BAT file until you reboot your computer. For more information, consult Chapter 8, "Configuring Your Personal Computer."*

To set PC DOS to look for application programs or commands in a different location, follow these steps:

1. Change to the root directory.

2. At the PC DOS command prompt, type the word **PATH**.

3. Press the **Spacebar** once.

4. Type the path to the directory where you want PC DOS to look for application programs or commands. The command line should look like the following:

```
C:\>PATH C:\DOS;C:\UTILS;C:\WINDOWS
```

The default path for PC DOS is PATH=C:\DOS

Note: *To add more than one location, separate each directory with a semicolon but no spaces. For example, to add both the DOS directory and the WINDOWS directory to the PATH command, type* **C:\DOS;C:\WINDOWS**.

5. Press **Enter**. PC DOS looks first in the DOS directory, then in the UTILS directory, and then in the WINDOWS directory.

Checking the System Memory

You need to know how much memory is available on your computer. Most application programs have minimum memory requirements, and you should make sure that your computer meets those requirements before you try to use the programs.

To find out how much memory is available on your computer and how the memory is allocated, follow these steps:

1. At the PC DOS command prompt, type **MEM**.

2. Press **Enter**. PC DOS displays a status report detailing your system memory.

Type the command here

By using the MEM command, you can see how much memory you have on your system, how the memory is allocated, and how much memory is available.

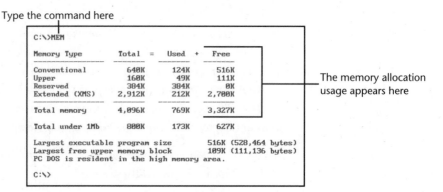

The memory allocation usage appears here

```
C:\>MEM

Memory Type        Total   =   Used   +   Free
-------------------------------------------------
Conventional        640K        124K       516K
Upper               160K         49K       111K
Reserved            384K        384K         0K
Extended (XMS)    2,912K        212K     2,700K
                 --------     -------    -------
Total memory      4,096K        769K     3,327K

Total under 1Mb     800K        173K       627K

Largest executable program size       516K (528,464 bytes)
Largest free upper memory block       109K (111,136 bytes)
PC DOS is resident in the high memory area.

C:\>
```

The MEM command displays information about different types of memory—conventional, upper, adapter RAM/ROM, extended, and expanded or reserved. (To learn more about memory and about optimizing the allocation of memory on your computer, see Chapter 8, "Configuring Your Personal Computer.")

Chapter 3

Working with the Windows Desktop

Graphical user interface
An easy-to-use method of combining graphics, menus, and plain English commands to let the user communicate with the computer.

Microsoft Windows is a powerful operating environment that enables you to access the power of PC DOS without memorizing PC DOS commands and syntax. Windows uses a *graphical user interface* (GUI) so that you can easily see on-screen the tools you need to complete specific file and program management tasks.

Windows provides many useful tools and accessories for managing your data and running your application programs. This chapter, an overview of the Windows environment, is designed to help you learn the basics of Windows, including starting Windows, identifying the different parts of the Windows desktop, and using the mouse to navigate through the desktop.

After you understand the basics of the Windows environment, you can move on to later chapters, which provide more detail on using Windows to accomplish specific tasks.

Starting Windows

To start Windows from the PC DOS command prompt, follow these steps:

1. Type **WIN**.

2. Press **Enter**. Windows begins loading. When it is loaded, you see the Program Manager window open on-screen.

Window
A rectangular area on-screen in which you view program icons, application programs, or documents.

The Program Manager *window* includes many different elements, such as the menu bar, title bar, and *icons*. Your Program Manager window may look different from the window used in this book's illustrations. For example, you may have different program group icons across the bottom of the Program Manager window.

The first time you start Windows, the IBM Tools program group window is usually open on the desktop.

The menu bar   The title bar   An open window

Program icons ⎯
The mouse pointer⎯

IBM AntiVirus	Backup	Scheduler
Undelete	PC DOS Prompt	

Program Manager

File   Options   Window   Help

IBM Tools

StartUp   Applications   Microsoft Office   Games   Main   Accessories   New Group

Program group icons   The desktop

Using a Mouse in Windows

Mouse
A pointing device used in many application programs to make choices, select data, and otherwise communicate with the computer.

Windows is designed for use with a *mouse*. Although you can get by with just a keyboard, using a mouse is much easier. This book assumes that you are using a mouse. If you are using a keyboard, consult your Windows User's Guide for more information.

In the Windows desktop, you can use a mouse to

- Open windows

- Close windows

- Open menus

■ Choose menu commands

■ Rearrange on-screen items, such as icons and windows

Note: *For more information about performing specific tasks in Windows, see Chapter 4, "Making Windows Work."*

The position of the mouse is indicated on-screen by a *mouse pointer.* Usually, the mouse pointer is an arrow, but it sometimes changes shape depending on the current action.

Mouse pad
A pad that provides a uniform surface for a mouse to slide on.

On-screen the mouse pointer moves according to the movements of the mouse on your desk or on a *mouse pad.* To move the mouse pointer, simply move the mouse.

3

There are three basic mouse actions:

■ *Click.* To point to an item and press and release quickly the left mouse button. You click to select an item, such as an option on a menu. To cancel a selection, click an empty area of the desktop.

■ *Double-click.* To point to an item and then press and release the left mouse button twice, as quickly as possible. You double-click to open or close windows and to start applications from icons.

■ *Drag.* To point to an item, press and hold the left mouse button as you move the pointer to another location, and then release the mouse button. You drag to resize windows, move icons, and scroll.

Note: *Unless otherwise specified, the left mouse button is used for all mouse actions.*

If you have problems...

If you try to double-click but nothing happens, you may not be clicking fast enough. Try again.

Understanding the Windows Desktop

Your screen provides a background for Windows, called a *desktop.* On the desktop, each application is displayed in its own window (hence the

Desktop
The background of the screen, on which windows, icons, and dialog boxes appear.

name Windows). All windows have the same set of controls that enable you to move, resize, and manipulate the window.

If you have multiple windows open, they may overlap on the desktop, just as papers on your desk can be stacked one on top of the other. The first time you start Windows, the IBM Tools program group window is usually open on top of the Program Manager window.

To use Microsoft Windows effectively, you should learn the different parts of the Windows desktop.

The Title Bar

Across the top of each window is its title bar. At the right side of the title bar are the Minimize button for reducing windows to icons and the Maximize button for expanding windows to fill the desktop. At the left side of the title bar is a box with a small hyphen in it, called the Control menu icon. The Control icon activates a window's Control menu.

Every open window has a title bar, used to identify the contents of the window.

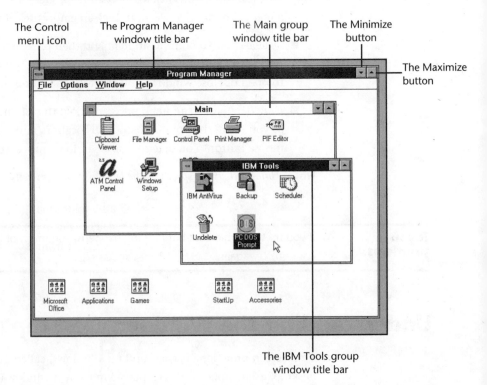

The Control menu icon

The Program Manager window title bar

The Main group window title bar

The Minimize button

The Maximize button

The IBM Tools group window title bar

Menus

Menus enable you to select options to perform functions or carry out commands. The Control menu enables you to control the size and position of its window, for example. Some windows have menu bars below the title bar. When you select an item from the menu bar, a menu drops down into the window.

Choose a menu command here

Menus, like the Control menu shown here, enable you to choose commands without remembering syntax, switches, or parameters.

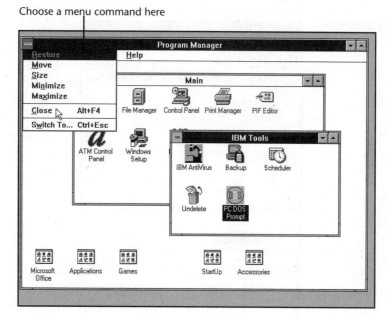

Dialog Boxes

Some menu options require you to enter additional information. When you select one of these options, a *dialog box* opens. You either type the additional information into a text box, select from a list of options, or select a button.

Enter additional information here

In a dialog box, you provide additional information that Windows needs to complete the command.

Buttons

Buttons are areas on the screen with which you select actions or commands. Most dialog boxes have at least a Cancel button, which stops the current activity and returns to the previous screen; an OK button, which accepts the current activity; and a Help button, which opens a Help window. Some windows have buttons, too. You can use the Minimize and Maximize buttons to control the size of the current window.

By using buttons, you can set options or choose commands.

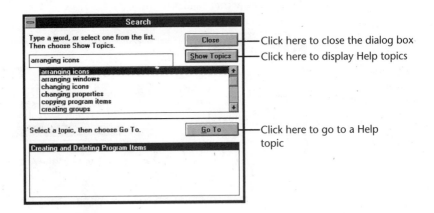

Click here to close the dialog box

Click here to display Help topics

Click here to go to a Help topic

Icons

Icons are small pictures used to identify groups of application programs files, or directories. You open windows, start application programs, and select items by selecting the appropriate icons.

Understanding the Program Manager

The Program Manager is the central Microsoft Windows program. When you start Microsoft Windows, the Program Manager starts automatically. When you exit Microsoft Windows, you exit the Program Manager. You cannot run Microsoft Windows if you are not running the Program Manager.

The Program Manager does what its name implies—it manages application programs. You use the Program Manager to organize application programs into groups called *program groups*, establishing a set which can be accessed through the same program group window. Usually, programs in a group are related, either by functionality or by usage (such as a gorup of accessories) or by usage (such as a group of application programs used to compile a monthly newsletter).

Each program group is represented by a program group icon.

When you double-click a program group icon, a group window opens on-screen.

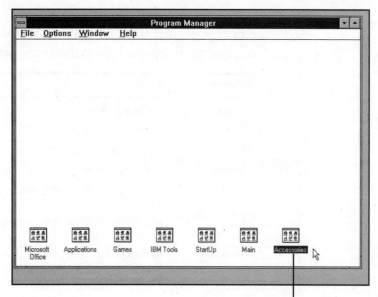

Double-click to open the Accessories group window

In each program group window, you see the icons for each individual program item in the group.

When you double-click a program icon, the accessory program starts.

Double-click to start Windows Paintbrush

Windows sets up some program groups automatically. You see their icons at the bottom of the Program Manager screen:

■ *Main program group.* Within this group, you find Microsoft Windows system application programs, which are programs that help you work with your system (computer). The Main program group includes the File Manager, Print Manager, DOS Prompt, Windows Setup, Control Panel, Clipboard, and other application program items.

■ *Accessories program group*. The Accessories program group contains accessory programs that are provided with Microsoft Windows. The following list includes some of these programs.

Program	Function
Calculator	Displays a calculator
Clock	Displays the time
Notepad	Enables you to enter, print, and edit notes
Calendar	Enables you to enter and review appointments
Cardfile	Enables you to enter, edit, sort, and delete cards in card file
Write	Enables you to create, edit, format, and print word processing documents
Paintbrush	Enables you to create, edit, and print drawings. Paintbrush is a complete drawing program.

Note: *For information about starting application programs and about using the Windows accessories, see Chapter 4, "Making Windows Work."*

■ *Games program group*. The Games program group contains two games: Solitaire and Minesweeper.

■ *StartUp group*. This group is empty until you add application programs to it. Applications you place in the StartUp group start when you enter Windows.

■ *Applications group*. When you install Microsoft Windows, the Setup program looks at the application programs on your hard disk. If you have any application programs that Microsoft Windows recognizes, Setup creates program icons for them and stores them in a group named Windows Applications. Setup also creates a group for Non-Windows Applications.

Exiting Windows

You should always exit Windows before turning off your computer. To exit Windows and return to the PC DOS command prompt, follow these steps:

1. Close all open windows and applications.

2. Point to **F**ile in the menu bar, and click the left mouse button.

3. Point to **E**xit Windows, and click the left mouse button. Windows asks you to confirm that you want to exit.

4. Point to OK, and click the left mouse button. Windows closes, and the PC DOS command prompt is displayed on-screen.

3

Tip
As a shortcut, simply double-click the Control menu button at the far left of the Program Manager title bar. Windows asks you to confirm that you want to exit. Click OK.

Chapter 4

Making Windows Work

Application program
A computer program designed to help you perform tasks such as writing a report. Also called application.

One of the primary benefits of Windows is that all Windows *application programs* use similar operating concepts. After you learn to use one Windows application program, you can use them all.

From the Windows desktop, you have access to the menus, icons, windows, and dialog boxes you need to manage programs and files. In this chapter, you learn to use the Program Manager to organize the desktop. You learn to control the size and position of windows and icons, to organize application programs into groups, and to start them. You even learn to use the PC DOS command prompt without turning off Windows. To make sure that you don't get stuck along the way, this chapter first presents how to display Help information for all Windows tasks.

Getting Help

Almost every Windows application program has a Help menu. From the Help menu, you can start a Help program to display information about many aspects of the application program.

To display Help information, take one of the following actions:

Context-sensitive
Pertaining to the current action.

■ Press **F1**. The Help program starts, and a *context-sensitive* Help window opens on-screen.

■ Choose **H**elp from the menu bar, and choose one of the Help menu commands.

If you have problems...   To choose a menu item, point to it with the mouse, and then click the left mouse button.

Displaying Help for a Topic

To display Help for a particular topic, follow these steps:

1. Choose **H**elp from the menu bar.

2. Choose **C**ontents from the Help menu. A Help Window opens; it displays the main topics for which Help is available.

The Help window groups topics into How To and Commands categories.

Choose a How To topic here

Choose a Commands topic here

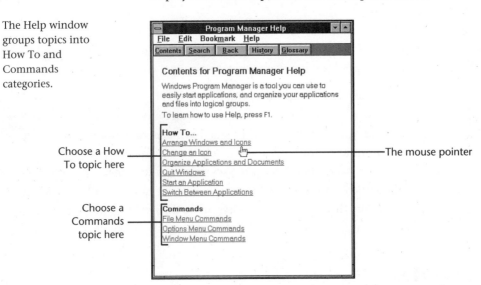

The mouse pointer

3. Choose the topic for which you want additional information. Windows displays the Help information.

The Control menu button

Choose to search for a Help topic

Most Windows
application
programs have
similar Help
programs. This
screen displays
Help for using the
Program Manager.
To scroll through
the Help screen,
click one of the
scroll arrows on
the right side of
the screen.

Click here to display the
Help table of contents

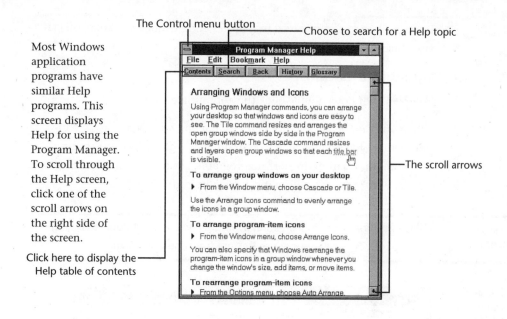

The scroll arrows

Note: *In the Help program, when the mouse pointer is on a topic for which you can get Help, the pointer changes to a hand with a pointing finger.*

Closing the Help Window

To close the Help window, take one of the following actions:

- Choose **C**lose from the Help window's Control menu.

- Choose E**x**it from the Help window's File menu.

- Double-click the Control menu button.

If you have problems... To open the Control menu, click the Control menu button at the far left end of the window's title bar.

Getting Comfortable with Windows

To be comfortable using Windows, you need to know how to control your Windows desktop, which in large part means controlling the windows themselves.

All the windows that appear in Windows, including the Program Manager, can be opened, closed, moved, and resized. In this section, you learn the basic tasks involved in manipulating windows so that you can easily access the information you need.

Opening a Window

To open a window, double-click the appropriate icon.

When you double-click a program group icon, you open a group window. When you double-click a program icon, you start that program. For more information on starting programs, see the section "Starting Application Programs Automatically," later in this chapter.

If you have problems... If a Control menu opens instead of a window, you are not double-clicking fast enough. Try again, or choose **R**estore from the Control menu.

You can continue opening windows until the desktop is full or until the computer runs out of memory.

The Games group window is open and active

Double-click here to open the Accessories group window

Don't worry if your screen looks different from the screens used to illustrate this book. Your desktop may be organized differently. You still can perform all the same tasks.

Note: *You can also use the Control menu to open a window. Click the icon to display the Control menu. Then click **R**estore.*

Changing the Active Window

Active window
The window in
which you are
currently working.

No matter how many windows are open on the desktop, you can work only in the *active window*.

You can tell which window is active in two ways:

- The active window is on the top of other open windows on the desktop.

- The title bar of the active window is highlighted.

Four windows are
open. The IBM
Tools group
window is the
active window.

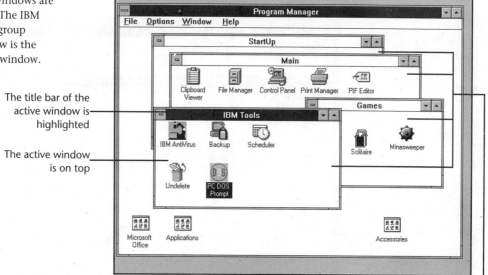

The title bar of the
active window is
highlighted

The active window
is on top

Open windows

To make a window active, click anywhere in it. The window moves to the top of the desktop, and its title bar appears in a different color or shade.

**If you have
problems...**

If the window you want to make active is hidden behind another window, click **W**indow on the menu bar to open the Window menu. From the list of available windows, choose the one you want to make active.

Resizing a Window

You can change the size of any open window by dragging its borders with the mouse.

To resize a window, follow these steps:

1. Point to the border you want to move.

Note: *When you are pointing to the border, the mouse pointer changes shape to a double-headed arrow.*

2. Press and hold down the left mouse button, and drag the border to its new location. As you drag, you see the border move along with the mouse pointer.

3. Release the mouse button. The window adjusts to the new size.

To resize a window, drag one of its borders.

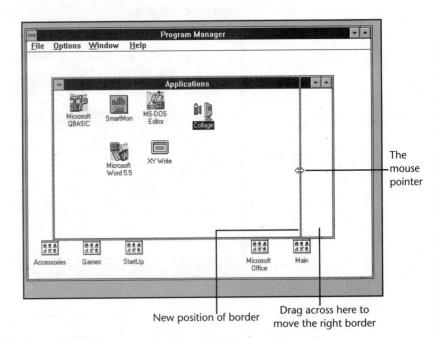

The mouse pointer

New position of border

Drag across here to move the right border

Note: *To change the height and width of the window simultaneously, drag one of the window's corners.*

If you have problems...

If nothing happens when you try to change a window size, you probably are not pointing at a border. Make sure that the mouse pointer changes to a double-headed arrow before you drag the border.

Note: *You can also resize a window by choosing **S**ize from its Control menu and using the arrow keys to move the borders. Press **Enter** when the window is the size you want.*

Moving a Window

You can move a window to a different location on the screen by dragging it with the mouse.

To move a window, follow these steps:

1. Point to the window's title bar.

2. Press and hold down the left mouse button, and drag the window to the new location. You see the borders of the window move with the mouse pointer.

3. Release the mouse button.

You can move a window to any location on the desktop.

Drag the title bar to move the window

The mouse pointer   New window position

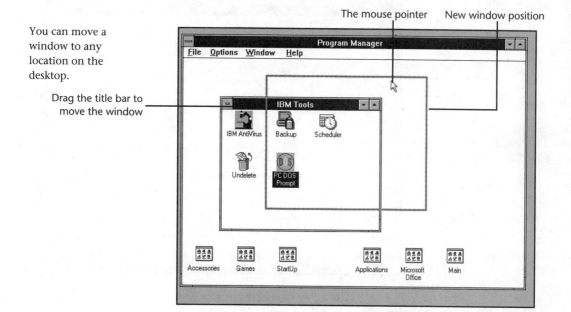

4

If you have problems...

If nothing happens when you try to move a window, you are probably not pointing to the window's title bar. Make sure that the mouse pointer is within the title bar before you drag the window.

Note: *You can also move a window by choosing* **M***ove from its Control menu and then using the arrow keys on the numeric keypad to move the window. Press* **Enter** *when the window is positioned as you want it.*

Maximizing a Window

Maximize
To increase the size
of a window until it
covers the desktop.

You can *maximize* a window to fill the entire desktop. Maximizing a window gives you more room to work.

To maximize a window, do one of the following:

- Click the Maximize button at the far right of the window's title bar. This button has an arrowhead pointing up.

- Choose **M**aximize from the window's Control menu.

Each window has a
Maximize button
at the right end of
its title bar.

Click here to maximize   Click here to maximize the
the IBM Tools window   Program Manager window

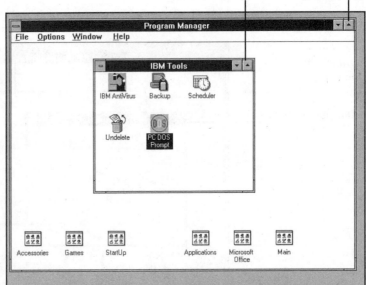

Minimizing a Window

Minimize
To reduce to
an icon.

You can *minimize* a window that you are not currently using.

To minimize a window, take one of the following actions:

- Click the Minimize button on the title bar. This button has an arrowhead pointing down.

- Choose Mi**n**imize from the window's Control menu.

The Minimize buttons

Each window has a
Minimize button
that you can use
to minimize the
window to an icon.

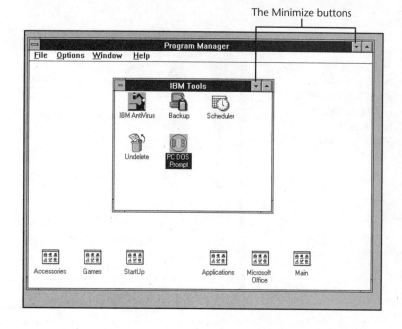

Note: *Program group windows, such as the Main group, are reduced to pro-*
gram group icons at the bottom of the Program Manager. Application program,
utility, or document icons are positioned at the bottom of the desktop, behind
any active windows. The application program that has been minimized is still
active; it is just out of the way.

Restoring a Window

Restore
To return a window
to its most recent
size and position
on the desktop.

You can *restore* a window that has been maximized or minimized to its
most recent size and location.

To restore a window to its previous size, take one of the following
actions:

■ Click the Restore button, which replaces the Maximize button
on the title bar. The Restore button has arrowheads pointing up
and down.

■ Choose **R**estore from the window's Control menu.

4

When you maximize a window, the Restore button appears at the left end of the title bar beneath the Maximize button.

The Restore button

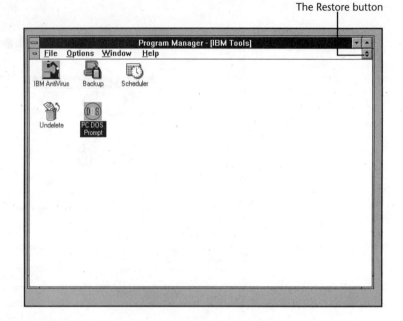

If you have problems...

If you try to restore the window but nothing happens, the window has not been maximized or minimized. You cannot restore a window unless it has been maximized or minimized first.

Arranging the Windows on Your Desktop

Tile
To arrange open windows on the desktop so that they do not overlap.

Cascade
To arrange open windows on the desktop so that they overlap, but at least a portion of each window is displayed.

Sometimes a desktop becomes so cluttered with open windows that you cannot tell what you are using. When that happens, you can choose either to *tile* or to *cascade* the open windows on-screen so that you can see them all.

To arrange the windows on the desktop, follow these steps:

1. Choose **W**indow from the menu bar to drop down the Window menu.

2. Choose one of the following:

    ■ **T**ile arranges the windows on-screen so that none are overlapping.

    ■ **C**ascade arranges the windows on-screen so that they overlap.

The windows are
tiled on the
desktop.

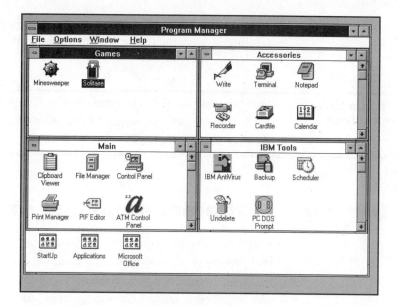

The windows are
cascaded on the
desktop.

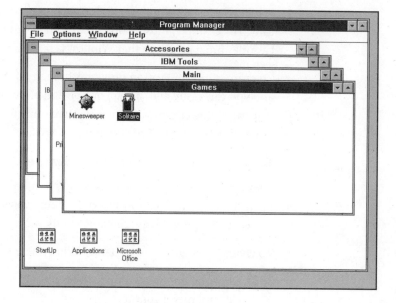

Closing a Window

To close a window, take one of the following actions:

■ Choose **C**lose from the window's Control menu.

■ Choose **C**lose from the window's File menu.

- Double-click the Control menu button. (To open the Control menu, click the Control menu button at the far left end of the window's title bar.)

If you have problems...	If the Exit Windows dialog box appears, you clicked the Control menu box for the Program Manager instead of the Control menu box for the window you want to close. Click Cancel.

Organizing Program Items and Groups

With Windows, you can organize application programs into groups so that you can easily find them. The groups appear on-screen in Group windows, from which you can launch application programs and complete other program and file management tasks.

When you install Windows, several program groups are created automatically. For example, most people have a Main program group and an Accessories program group that Windows created.

You can group application programs in many different combinations, and you can easily add, delete, or move them from groups. You can even place application programs in more than one group without keeping more than one copy of the program on disk.

Changing a Program Group Name

Below every program group icon is the program group's name. When you open the program group window, the name appears in the title bar. You can change a program group name at any time.

To change a program group name, follow these steps:

1. Click the program group icon to select it. The program group's Control menu appears.

2. Click File in the Program Manager menu bar to open the File menu. Don't worry that the Control menu disappears. You do not need it now.

3. Choose Properties from the File menu. The Program Group Properties dialog box appears. Inside this box, you see two text boxes:

Description and Group File. The Description text box contains the current program group name. (The mouse pointer is positioned inside this box.)

In the Program Group Properties dialog box, you can change the name of the selected program group.

4. In the **D**escription text box, type the new program group name.

5. Choose OK, or press **Enter**. You see the new name below the program group icon.

Adding a New Program Group

Windows creates some program groups during Setup. You can add a new program group at any time.

To add a new program group, follow these steps:

1. Close all program group windows.

2. Choose **F**ile from the menu bar to open the File menu.

3. Choose **N**ew from the File menu. You see the New Program Object dialog box. The Program **G**roup option is selected.

In the New Program Object dialog box, you choose to add a new program group.

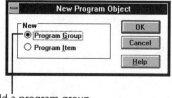

Choose to add a program group

If you have problems...

If Program **I**tem is selected instead of Program **G**roup, you did not close all program group windows before choosing **F**ile, **N**ew. Windows assumes that you want to add a program item to the active group window. Choose Cancel. Close all windows, and then try again.

---

4. Click OK. You see the Program Group Properties dialog box. Inside this box, you see two text boxes: **D**escription and **G**roup File.

In the Program Group Properties dialog box, you enter a name for the new program group.

Type the new program group name here

Program Group Properties
Description:		OK
Group File:		Cancel
		Help

5. In the **D**escription text box, type a name for the new program group.

6. Click OK. Windows opens the new program group window on-screen. (Windows inserts the path into the Group File text box.)

The new program group contains no program icons yet, but the program group name appears in the window's title bar.

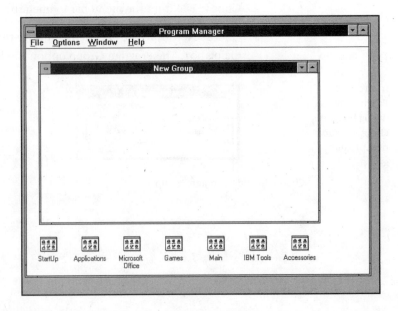

Moving a Program to a Different Group

To move program items from one group to another, follow these steps:

1. Open the group window that contains the item you want to move.

2. Open the group window to which you want to move the item.

3. Arrange the windows so that you can see them both on-screen.

Note: *You can arrange the windows by resizing and moving them or by tiling them on the desktop.*

4. Point to the icon for the item you want to move.

5. Press and hold down the mouse button and drag the icon to the other window.

6. Release the mouse button.

You can easily drag an icon from one window to another.

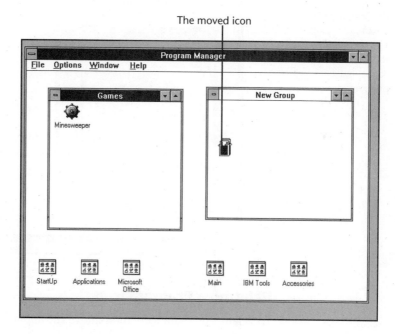

The moved icon

Copying a Program Item to Another Group

You can place a program item in more than one group.

To copy a program item from one group into another group, follow these steps:

1. Open the program group window that contains the program item you want to copy.

2. Open the program group window to which you want to copy the program item.

3. Arrange the windows so that you can see them both on-screen.

4. Point to the icon you want to copy.

5. Press and hold down **Ctrl**.

6. Press and hold down the mouse button, and drag the icon to the other program group window.

7. Release the mouse button and **Ctrl**.

The copied icon appears in both the new group and the original group. The program it represents is now part of both program groups.

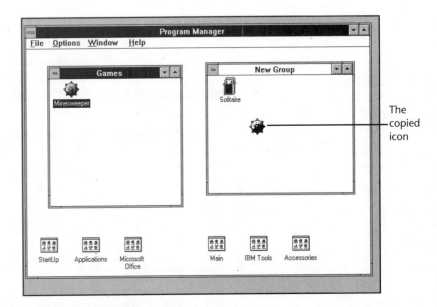

The copied icon

Deleting a Program Icon

To delete a program icon and remove the application program from that group, follow these steps:

1. Open the group window that contains the program icon you want to delete.

2. Click the icon you want to delete.

3. Choose **F**ile, **D**elete from the File menu. The Delete dialog box appears.

Windows asks for confirmation before deleting an icon.

4. Choose **Y**es to confirm that you want to delete the selected icon.

Tip

To remove an application program from a group quickly, drag the icon out of the group window and on to the desktop. When you see a No symbol (a circle with a slash through it), release the mouse button. The icon disappears.

Note: *When you delete a program item icon, you don't delete the program files on disk. The files are still there, but the item is no longer part of the program group.*

You can delete a program group icon using the same methods you use to delete a program item icon. When you delete a program group icon, all item icons in that group are also deleted.

Adding a New Program Icon

To add a new program item to a program group, follow these steps:

1. Open the program group window to which you want to add a new program item.

2. Choose **F**ile, **N**ew from the File menu. The New Program Object dialog box appears. The Program **I**tem option is selected.

In the New
Program Object
dialog box, choose
to create a new
program item.

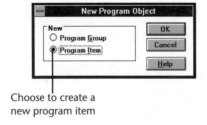

Choose to create a
new program item

3. Click OK. You see the Program Item Properties dialog box. Inside this box, you see these text boxes: **D**escription, **C**ommand Line, **W**orking Directory, and **S**hortcut Key.

Type a name here

In the Program
Item Properties
dialog box, you
specify a name and
start-up options
for the new
program item.

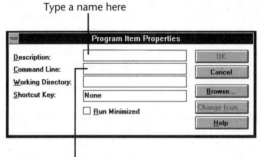

Type the command that PC DOS
uses to start the program here

4. In the **D**escription text box, type the name you want to appear below the icon in the program group window.

This step enters a name for the new application program and moves the insertion point to the **C**ommand Line text box.

5. In the **C**ommand Line text box, type the command that starts the application program from the PC DOS command prompt. If necessary, include the complete path to the application program, including the name of the directory containing the application program. (For information about the command used to start the application program, consult its documentation. For information about paths, see Chapter 1, "Understanding System Basics.")

6. Choose OK.

> **Tip**
>
> To move from one text box to another, click the mouse pointer in the text box, or press **Tab**.

Note: *Adding an application program isn't always easy. You have to know the command name and know where that file is kept on your hard disk.*

Arranging Icons within a Window

You can move and rearrange icons on the desktop. To move an icon, follow these steps:

1. Point to the icon you want to move.

2. Press and hold down the left mouse button.

3. Drag the icon to the new location.

To arrange all icons neatly within a window, follow these steps:

1. Make the window that contains the icons active.

2. Choose **W**indow from the menu bar to drop down the Window menu.

3. Choose **A**rrange Icons.

Changing an Application Program's Icon

Windows comes with a selection of icons and usually automatically assigns icons to new program items and program groups. You can select a different icon at any time, however.

To change an application program's icon, follow these steps:

1. Open the program group that contains the icon you want to change.

2. Choose the icon you want to change.

3. Choose **F**ile, **P**roperties. You see the Program Item Properties dialog box.

In the Program Item Properties dialog box, you can see the current program item icon and choose a different icon.

The current icon

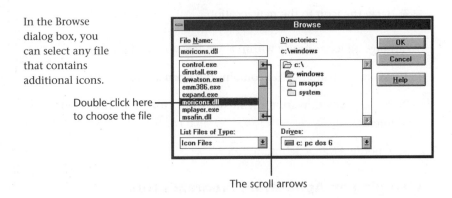

4. In the Program Item Properties dialog box, click the Change **I**con button. The Change Icon dialog box appears.

5. In the Change Icon dialog box, click the **B**rowse button. The Browse dialog box appears.

6. In the Browse dialog box, scroll through the File **N**ame list until you see the file MORICONS.DLL.

In the Browse dialog box, you can select any file that contains additional icons.

Double-click here to choose the file

The scroll arrows

7. Double-click the MORICONS file to select it. The icons are displayed in the Change Icon dialog box.

8. In the **C**urrent Icon text box, choose the icon you want to use.

Use the scroll arrow below the Current Icon text box to scroll through the list of icons.

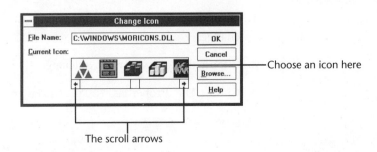

Choose an icon here

The scroll arrows

9. Choose OK to return to the Program Item Properties dialog box.

10. Choose OK to assign the new icon to the program item.

Running Application Programs in Windows

In Windows, application programs run within application windows. To run an application program, you open its window. You can have more than one window open at a time, although you can work only in the active window.

There are many different ways to open application windows in Windows. In this section, you learn to start application programs and to switch among them.

Starting an Application Program by Using Its Icon

The fastest way to start an application program in Windows is to use its program item icon.

To start an application program from a program item icon, follow these steps:

1. Open the program group window that contains the application program you want to start.

2. Double-click the program item icon. A small hourglass on-screen indicates that Windows is starting the application program.

Double-click here to start
Word for Windows

You can quickly start an application program by double-clicking its program item icon.

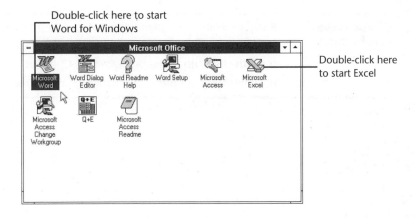

Double-click here
to start Excel

If you have problems...	If the application program doesn't start, you probably did not click twice. Point to the icon again, and press the mouse button twice in rapid succession.

Running an Application Program from the File Menu

You can use the File menu to run any application program, even if it has not been added to a program group. You can run application programs from diskettes or from the hard disk.

To start an application program by using the File menu, follow these steps:

1. Choose **F**ile, **R**un. The Run dialog box appears.

You can run any program by typing its command line in the Run dialog box.

2. In the **C**ommand Line text box, type the command you use to start the application program from the PC DOS command prompt. If necessary, enter the full path to the program files.

3. Click OK. Windows starts loading the application program.

If you have problems...	If the application program doesn't start, you probably did not type the correct command line. Check your spelling, and make sure that you have entered the full path to the program files. Consult the application program's documentation for more information on the correct command.

Running More Than One Application Program Simultaneously

One of the benefits of Windows is that you can run application programs simultaneously. Each application program runs in its own window; you can switch back and forth among the open application programs and even copy information from one application program to another.

To start more than one application program, follow these steps:

1. Start the first application program, using any of the methods described in the preceding sections.

2. Take one of the following actions to return to the Program Manager:

■ Press **Alt+Tab**.

■ Press **Ctrl+Esc** to display the Task List. Choose Program Manager, and then choose **S**witch To.

■ Click within the Program Manager window if you can see it on-screen.

To return to the Program Manager to start another application program, click within the Program Manager window.

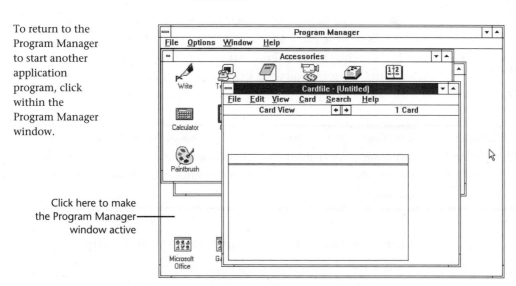

Click here to make the Program Manager window active

3. Open another application program, using any of the methods described in the preceding sections.

Switching among Open Application Programs

You can switch among open application programs by using any of the following methods:

- If you can see the application program window on-screen, click in it. It becomes the active window.

- Press **Ctrl+Esc** to display the Task List. Choose the application program you want to make active, and then choose **S**witch To.

Use the Task List to change among open application programs.

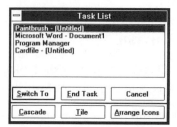

- Press and hold down the **Alt** key, and then press the **Tab** key to display the name and icon of the next open application program. Continue holding down **Alt** and pressing **Tab** until the application program you want to make active is displayed; release the Alt and Tab keys.

If you have problems...

If nothing happens when you press **Alt+Tab**, Application Fast Alt+Tab Switching is not enabled. See your Windows documentation for more information. In the meantime, try one of the other methods described in this section.

Starting Application Programs Automatically

If you want an application program to start automatically whenever you start Windows, you can add that application program to the StartUp program group. Windows starts all programs in the StartUp program group each time you start Windows.

To add application programs to the StartUp program group, follow these steps:

1. Open the group window that contains the program item you want to start automatically.

2. Open the StartUp program group window.

Windows automatically starts all programs in the StartUp program group each time Windows starts.

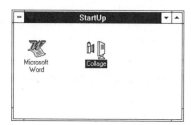

3. Arrange the windows so that you can see them both on-screen.

4. Copy the icon for the application program you want to start automatically to the StartUp program group window. For more information, see the section "Copying a Program Item to Another Group," earlier in this chapter.

Exiting an Application Program

Most Windows application programs use the same exit procedures. For specific information about a particular application program, consult its documentation.

To exit a Windows application program, take one of the following actions:

■ Double-click the application program window's Control menu button.

■ Choose **F**ile, E**x**it.

■ Press **Alt+F4**

Usually, the program prompts you to save any changes you have made.

Note: *Be sure to exit all application programs before exiting Windows.*

Using Windows Accessories

Windows accessories are programs that can augment and enhance your Windows application programs. You can leave accessories open or minimized while you use other application programs so that you can access them quickly and easily. You can maximize any accessory window to provide more room for working.

During Setup, Windows places the accessories programs in a program group called Accessories.

To see the icons for the accessories, open the Accessories group window.

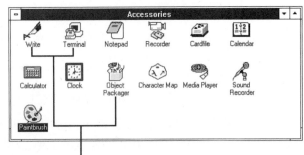

Double-click its icon to start an Accessories program

Accessories perform different functions, but they operate in a manner similar to the operation of other Windows application programs.

Starting and Using an Accessory

To start most accessories, open the Accessories group window and double-click the accessory icon.

To open a new file in an accessory, select **N**ew from the File menu. A new, untitled file opens.

To open an existing file in an accessory program, follow these steps:

1. Choose **F**ile, **O**pen. The Open dialog box appears.

2. In the Open dialog box, select the name of the file you want to open. If necessary, select the drive and directory first. Most accessories are associated with a specific file extension, but you can display and select files with different extensions by using the List Files of **T**ype drop-down list.

3. Choose OK.

Note: *You can open only one file at a time in Windows accessories. When you open a new file, the file you were working in closes. To open another file in the same accessory, go back to the Program Manager and double-click the icon.*

Saving an Accessory File

To save a file while in an accessory, follow these steps:

1. Choose File, Save. If you are saving a file for the first time, the Save As dialog box appears.

2. Enter the file name. If necessary, enter the drive and directory where you want to store the file.

3. Choose OK.

Note: *To save an accessory file with a new name, choose File, Save As.*

Printing an Accessory File

To print a file in an accessory, follow these steps:

1. Choose Print Setup to select a printer and set printer options.

2. Choose File, Print.

Closing an Accessory

To exit an accessory, take one of the following actions:

- Choose File, Exit.

- Double-click the Control menu button on the title bar.

- Choose Close from the Control menu.

If you have not saved changes to the current file, a dialog box asks whether you want to save your changes before closing.

Exploring the Accessories

Most Windows accessories come standard with Windows. Some, however, are available only if your system can use them. For example, Chat, WinMeter, and Net Watcher are present only on networked systems. Media Player and Sound Recorder can be used only on multimedia computers. Following are descriptions of some of the accessories.

Windows Write

Write is a word processing accessory designed specifically for Windows. This accessory uses the Windows environment to simplify basic editing, formatting, and text-management tasks. Write also enables you to link text with data from other Windows application programs.

To start Write, select the Write icon from the Program Manager Accessories group window.

The Write window opens with a new, untitled document file displayed.

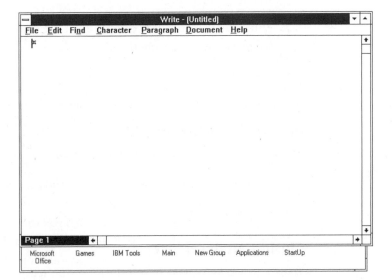

Windows Paintbrush

Paintbrush is a graphics accessory that enables you to create pictures that can be used by themselves or incorporated into other Windows application programs.

To start Paintbrush, select the Paintbrush icon from the Program Manager Accessories group window.

The Paintbrush window opens with a new, untitled file displayed.

Select a tool here—

Select a line-width here—

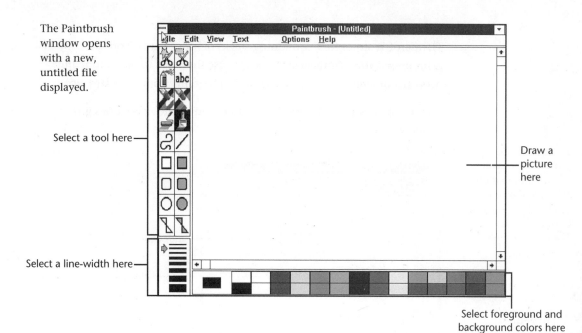

Draw a picture here

Select foreground and background colors here

4

Notepad

The Notepad is a limited text editor, which you can use to open, edit, and save text files. Notepad cannot hold graphics files. You can use the Notepad to jot notes and to store text you want to move from one application program to another.

To start the Notepad, choose the Notepad icon in the Accessories group window.

The Notepad window opens with a new, untitled file displayed.

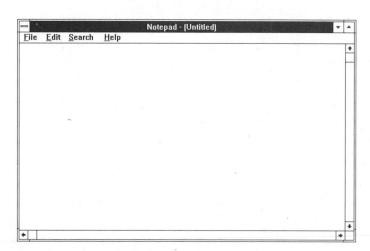

Cardfile

The Cardfile stores files containing stacks of index cards. You can copy or print information from a card. You can use the cards to dial phone numbers on a modem or to start application programs from *embedded objects*.

To start the Cardfile, choose the Cardfile icon in the Accessories group window.

In Cardfile, enter card information below the double line. Enter the title or index information above the double line.

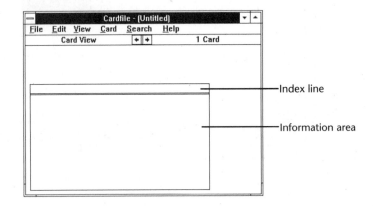

Index line

Information area

Embedded object

An element copied from one application program into another one, such as a spreadsheet in Excel placed into a document in Word.

Calendar

Use the Calendar to set appointments, mark special days, and issue an alarm. To open the Calendar, choose the Calendar icon from the Accessories group window.

When you open the Calendar, the daily view is displayed, marked in hourly intervals. Select **M**onth from the View menu to display the monthly view.

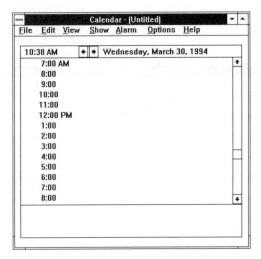

Calculator

Use the Calculator to perform mathematical and scientific calculations. With the mouse, click the keys in the Calculator window. With a keyboard, press the corresponding key on the keyboard. Special function keys are the following:

Keyboard Key Functions		
Keys	**Function**	**Calculator Keys**
Ctrl+L	Clear memory	MC
Ctrl+R	Display memory	MR
Ctrl+P	Add to memory	M+
Ctrl+M	Store value in memory	MS
Del	Delete displayed value	CE
Backspace	Delete last digit in displayed value	Back
F9	Change sign	+/-
@	Square root	sqrt
R	Calculate reciprocal	1/x
Esc	Clear	C

4

Use the Calculator to perform mathematical functions while you work.

Clock

Open the Clock to check the time. Use the Settings menu to change the appearance of the clock. To set the time, use the Date/Time item in the Windows Control Panel.

Minimize the Clock window to keep it displayed on the desktop while you work.

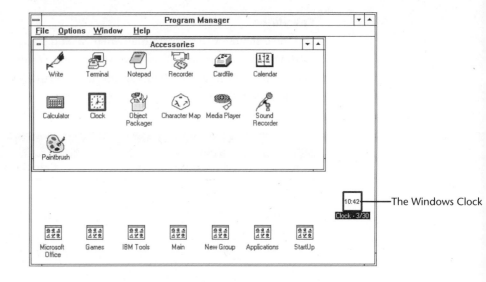

The Windows Clock

Using the Windows Clipboard

Another Windows feature worth mentioning is the Clipboard. The Clipboard is a temporary storage area that you can use to copy selected text or objects among any Windows accessory or application program files. You must use the Clipboard from within any Windows application program—it does not run in its own window.

To copy selected text or objects from any file to the Clipboard, select the item in the file, and then choose **E**dit, **C**opy.

To copy text or objects from the Clipboard into a file, open the file, position the cursor where you want the item placed, and then choose **E**dit, **P**aste.

Caution

The Clipboard can hold only one item at a time. As soon as you copy another item to the Clipboard, the previous item is deleted.

To view and save the item currently stored in the Clipboard, use the Clipboard Viewer. To open the Clipboard Viewer, double-click the Clipboard Viewer icon from the Main group window, not from the Accessories group window.

The Clipboard is a useful feature in Windows. You also can use it to link and embed objects from one application program to another.

Accessing the PC DOS Command Prompt

You can access the PC DOS command prompt without closing Windows. To access the PC DOS command prompt, follow these steps:

1. Open the IBM Tools program group window.

Double-click the PC DOS Prompt icon to return temporarily to the PC DOS command prompt.

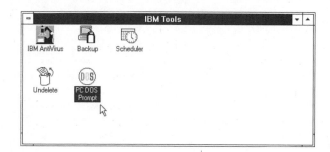

2. Double-click the PC DOS Prompt icon. You see the PC DOS command prompt displayed on-screen.

To return to Windows, follow these steps:

1. At the PC DOS command prompt, type **EXIT**.

2. Press **Enter**.

Note: *When Windows is running, do not type* **WIN** *to start it again.*

Chapter 5

Using File Manager

In Chapter 1, "Understanding System Basics," you learned how PC DOS uses files and directories to organize data on a disk. In Chapter 2, "Making PC DOS Work," you learned to use PC DOS commands to manage your files, directories, and disks.

Windows has a built-in program designed to help you visualize the organization of the information you have stored on disks. With Windows File Manager, you can view your disk organization on-screen and group your directories and files in an organization you can understand.

In this chapter, you learn to use the File Manager to control your disks, files, and directories.

Opening the File Manager

The File Manager, like any other Windows application program, runs in its own window. You use the techniques covered in detail in Chapter 4, "Making Windows Work," to control the File Manager window.

To open the File Manager, follow these steps:

1. Double-click the Main group icon to open the window.

The File Manager
icon looks like a
two-drawer file
cabinet.

Double-click here to
start the File Manager

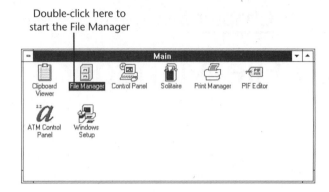

2. Double-click the File Manager icon. The File Manager opens
on-screen.

Note: *To allow more space within the File Manager for viewing files,*
maximize the File Manager window.

The maximized
File Manager
window covers the
Program Manager
window on the
desktop.

The menu bar

The Control
menu button

The title bar

The current
directory path

Disk icons

The directory tree

The status line

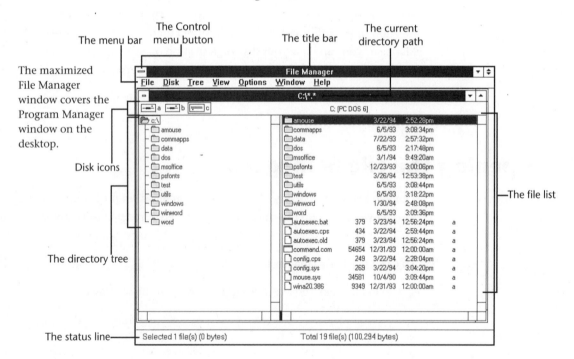

The file list

At the top of the File Manager window, you see the title bar and the
menu bar. Below the menu bar, you see a window that displays icons for
the available drives, a directory list, and a file list. The name of the current directory appears in the title bar of this window.

On the status line at the bottom of the File Manager window, you see the number of bytes free, total bytes, and total number of files for the current directory.

In the File Manager, directories are indicated by folder icons, and files are indicated by document icons. Program files are indicated by window icons.

The left side of the window shows the directory list and is called the directory tree window.

The selected directory

Folder icons

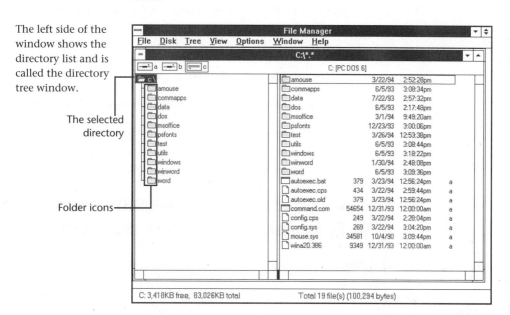

The right side of the window displays the subdirectories and files in the selected directory and is called the file list area.

Program icons

Document icons

Folder icons

The selected file

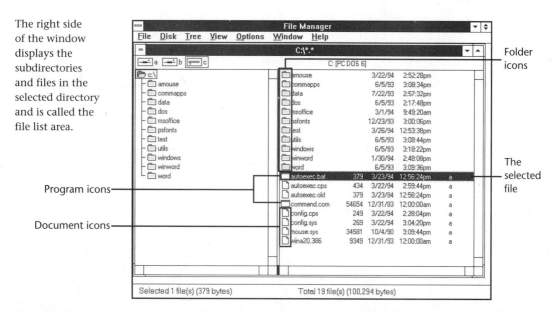

5

Note: *Your computer screen probably will look different from the screen used to illustrate this book because your hard disk will have different files and directories.*

Changing Drives

Active drive
The drive in which you are currently working.

In the File Manager, the directory tree area shows the directories stored on the *active drive*. If you want to work with directories and files stored on a different drive, you must change the active drive.

To make a different drive active, follow these steps:

1. Make sure that a diskette is in the drive you want to make active.

2. Click the diskette drive icon for the drive you want to make active. The directory tree and file list areas change to display the information on the diskette in the selected drive.

In this window, drive B is the active drive.

The drive icon ——

The current directory path ——

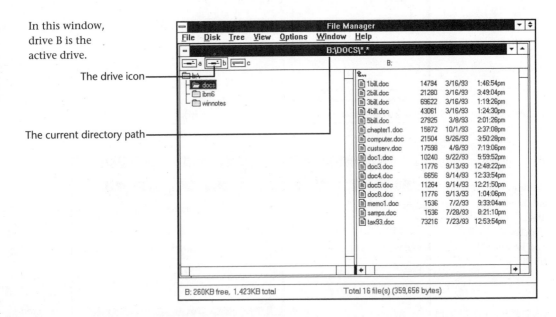

Opening Multiple Directory Windows

In the File Manager, you can open several directory windows at the same time. Each directory window can display different information. This capability is useful for seeing the contents of more than one directory or more than one disk.

To open an additional directory window, follow these steps:

1. Choose **W**indow from the menu bar to show the Window menu.

2. Choose **N**ew Window from the Window menu. A second window opens on top of the first window.

At first, the second window displays the same information as the first window. Later in this chapter, you learn how to change the information in the window.

The new window

The original window

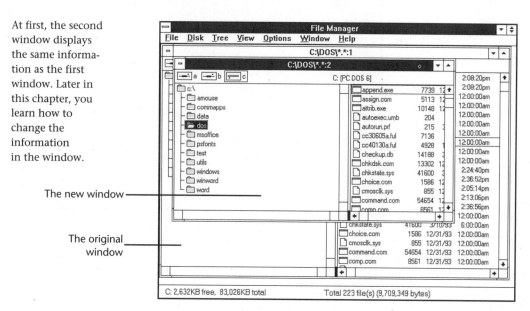

Note: *To open an additional window quickly, double-click the drive icon for the disk you want to be active in the new window.*

Arranging the Windows On-Screen

When you are working with more than one directory window open in the File Manager, you will usually want to be able to see the contents of them all.

To arrange the windows on-screen so that you can see the contents of each, follow these steps:

1. Open the windows.

2. Choose **W**indow from the menu bar to show the Window menu.

3. Choose **T**ile from the Window menu.

You can tile the windows on-screen so that they do not overlap.

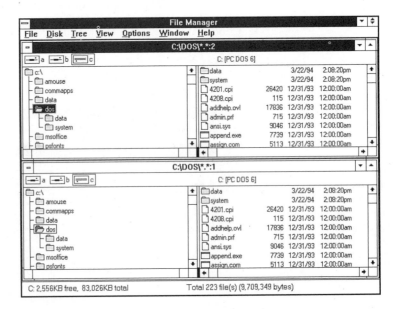

Opening a Directory

The file list area displays the files for the selected, or open, directory.

To open a directory, simply click the directory's folder icon in the directory tree. The folder icon opens, and the files contained in the directory are displayed in the file list area.

UTILS is the open
directory, and the
files contained
in the UTILS
directory are
displayed.

The open folder icon

The current directory
path

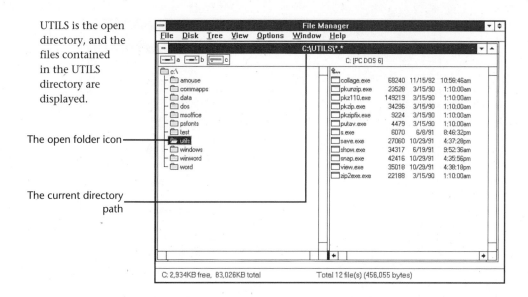

Expanding Directories

Expand

To display all the
subdirectories for a
selected directory or
for the whole direc-
tory tree.

You can *expand* the directory tree to display subdirectories. You can expand only one directory, or you can expand all directories.

To expand a directory, double-click the directory's folder icon. The folder
opens, and the subdirectories are displayed.

**If you have
problems...**

If the folder opens but the subdirectories do not appear, you did not double-
click fast enough. Try again.

5

The PC DOS directory has been expanded to display subdirectories.

PC DOS directory folder—

Subdirectories—

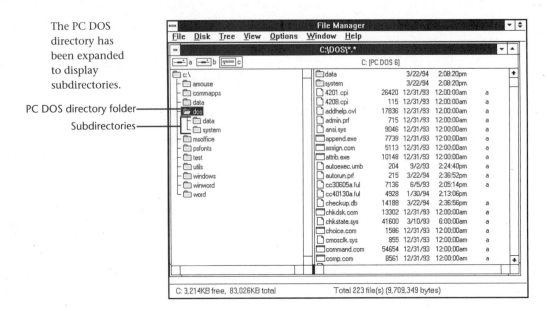

To expand all directories, follow these steps:

1. Choose **T**ree from the menu bar.

2. Choose Expand **A**ll from the **T**ree menu.

All directories and subdirectories on drive C are displayed in the directory tree area.

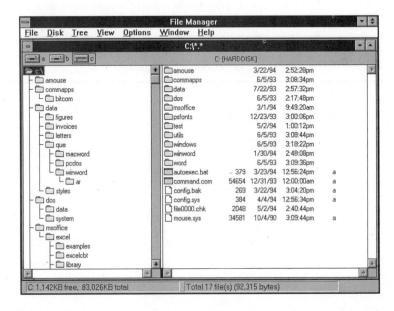

Collapse

To hide sub-directories for a directory or directory tree.

The root directory has been collapsed. All subdirectories of the root are hidden on the directory tree.

Collapsing Directories

You can *collapse* any expanded directory to hide the subdirectory folders.

To collapse a directory, double-click the directory's folder icon.

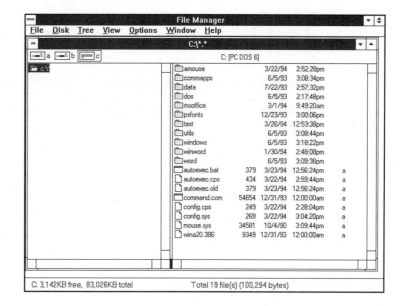

Changing the File Manager View

View

The way information in a utility or application program is displayed on-screen.

When you open the File Manager the first time, it appears in the default *view*. Both the directory tree and file list are displayed. You can change the way the File Manager displays information.

To change the File Manager view, follow these steps:

1. Choose **V**iew from the menu bar to show the View menu. The current view options are indicated on the View menu by check marks.

2. From the **V**iew menu, choose any of the following:

    ■ T**r**ee and Directory. To display both the directory tree and the file list. (This setting is the default.)

    ■ Tr**ee** Only. To display only the directory tree area.

5

- Directory **O**nly. To display only the file list area.

- Sp**l**it. To change the location of the split between the file list area and the directory tree area. You can drag the split line to any location.

Note: *For more information on the other options on the View menu, see the next section, "Changing the File List."*

The view has been changed to display only the directory tree area.

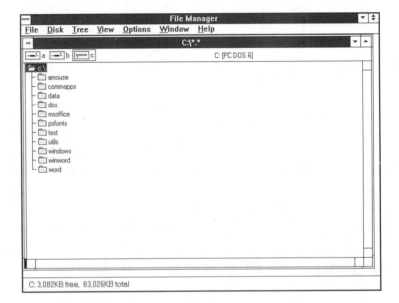

Changing the File List

You can change the file list in several ways: you can display only certain information about the files; you can sort the files in a different order; and you can display only certain files. The following sections explain how you can make these changes.

Displaying Specific Items of File Information

By default, the File Manager lists files alphabetically by name and displays all file information, including file name and extension, the time and date when the file was last modified, and the file size in bytes. You can choose what file information you want displayed.

To choose the file information you want displayed in the file list, follow these steps:

1. Choose **V**iew from the menu bar to show the View menu.

2. From the View menu, choose one of the following options:

- **N**ame. To display only file names in the file list area.

- **A**ll File Details. To display all file information in the file list area.

- **P**artial Details. To choose what file information you want to display.

File attribute

A term referring to four classifications of DOS files—hidden, read-only, archive, or system.

In the Partial Details dialog box, you can specify which file details you want to display.

If you choose Partial Details, the Partial Details dialog box appears. In the Partial Details dialog box, you can choose to display file size, the last date the file was modified, the last time the file was modified, or the *file attributes*, including whether the file is a hidden file, a read-only file, an archived file, or a system file.

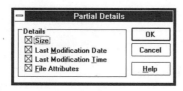

Sorting the File List

You can change the order of the file list. This feature is useful when you have many files and want certain files to appear near the top of the list.

To change the sort order of the files in the file list, follow these steps:

1. Choose **V**iew from the menu bar to show the View menu.

2. From the View menu, choose one of the following:

- **S**ort by Name. To list the files alphabetically by file name.

- Sort **b**y Type. To list files by type of file extension.

- Sort by Si**z**e. To list files according to size in bytes.

■ Sort by **D**ate. To list files according to date stamp.

■ By File **T**ype. To display only specified files. See the next
section "Displaying Specific Files" for more detail.

In this window,
the view has
been changed to
display only the
file list area with
the files sorted by
size—largest to
smallest.

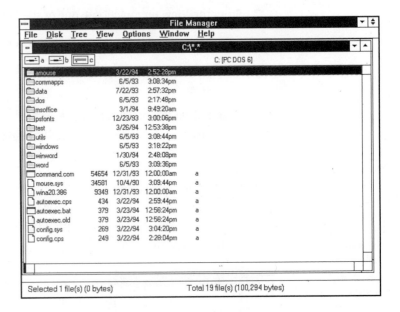

Displaying Specific Files

You can choose which files you want to include in the file list by using
wild-card characters to specify a group of files.

To display only specified files, follow these steps:

1. Choose **V**iew from the menu bar to show the View menu.

2. Choose By File **T**ype from the View menu. The By File Type dialog
box appears.

Type the file specification here

In the By File Type
dialog box, you
can specify the
types of files you
want to display.

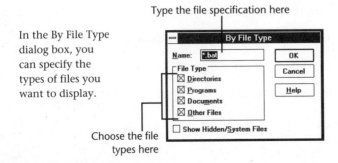

Choose the file
types here

3. In the **N**ame text box, type a file specification for the files you want to display. Use wild-card characters to specify a group of files. For example, type ***.TXT** to display all files with a TXT extension.

4. In the File Type area, choose the check boxes beside the types of files you want to display.

5. Click OK. The file list area changes to display only the files that match the file specification you entered.

In this window, only files matching the file specification *.BAT are displayed.

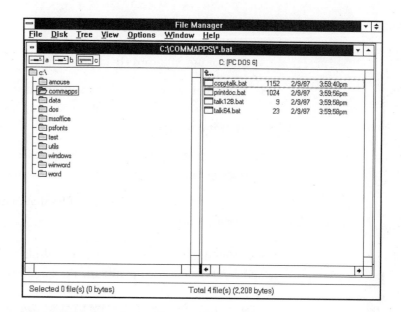

Searching for a File

If you forget where a file is located, you can use the File Manager to search for it. Even if you are not sure of the file name, you can use wild-card characters to find a group of files.

To search for a file, follow these steps:

1. Choose **F**ile, Sear**ch**. The Search dialog box appears.

Type the file specification here

You can use the
Search dialog box
to search for a file
anywhere on a
disk.

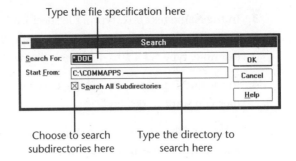

Choose to search
subdirectories here

Type the directory to
search here

2. In the **S**earch For text box, type the name of the file you want to find, or use wild-card characters to specify a group of files.

3. In the Start **F**rom text box, type the name of the directory that you want to search. The box probably already shows the name of the current directory.

4. To search all subdirectories of the specified directory, make sure that the Se**a**rch All Subdirectories check box has an x in it.

5. Choose OK. Windows looks for files that match the file specification.

When Windows completes the search, it displays the Search Results window. All the files that match the file specification are listed.

In the Search
Results window,
you see all the files
that match the file
specification you
entered.

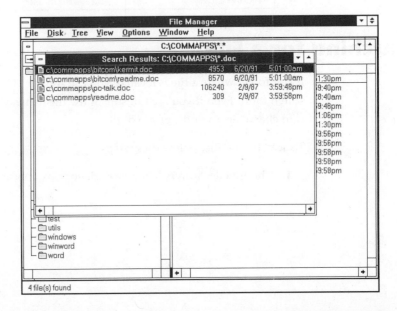

Note: *To close the Search Results window, double-click its Control menu button.*

Working with Files

You can use the File Manager to work with files in many ways. You must select a file before you can perform any action on it. After the file is selected, you can rename, move, copy, or delete it, as explained in the following sections.

Selecting Files

You can select one file or groups of files. Selected files are highlighted in the file list area.

To select a single file, click its icon in the file list area.

To select more than one file, follow these steps:

1. Click the icon of the first file you want to select.

2. Press and hold down **Ctrl**.

3. Click the icon of the next file you want to select.

4. Continue holding down **Ctrl** and clicking the icons to select the files.

5. When you have selected all the files you want, release the **Ctrl** key.

If you have problems...	If the first file you selected becomes unselected when you click another file, you are not holding down the **Ctrl** key. Try again.

Selected files are
highlighted in
the file list.

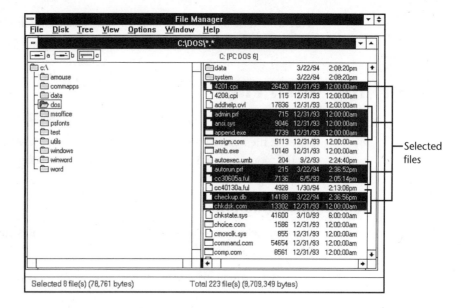

Copying Files

With two windows open on-screen, you can easily copy files from one
location to another. You can copy files to another disk or to a different
directory on the same disk.

To copy a file to another disk, follow these steps:

1. In one window, open the directory that contains the file you want
   to copy.

2. In another window, open the disk drive and the directory in which
   you want to place the copied file. Refer to the section "Opening
   Multiple Directory Windows," earlier in this chapter, for more information on displaying two directory windows.

3. Select the file you want to copy.

4. Drag the icon to the directory where you want to place the copied
   file. Notice that the file icon moves along with the mouse pointer.
   If you are copying more than one file, more than one file icon
   appears.

You can copy a file
by dragging it
from one directory
window to
another.

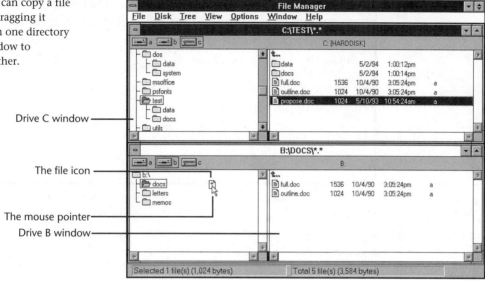

Drive C window ——

The file icon ——

The mouse pointer——
Drive B window——

5. Release the mouse button. The File Manager displays the Confirm
Mouse Operation dialog box.

6. Confirm that the file is being copied to the correct location, and
then click **Y**es.

5

In the Confirm
Mouse Operation
dialog box, make
sure that the file is
being copied to
the correct disk
and directory.

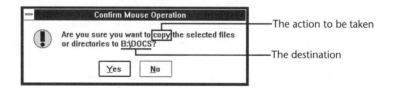

The action to be taken

The destination

To copy a file to a directory on the same disk, follow these steps:

1. In one window, open the directory that contains the file you want
to copy.

2. In another window, make sure that the directory in which you
want to place the copied file is displayed.

3. Select the file you want to copy.

4. Press and hold down **Ctrl**, and drag the icon to the directory where you want to place the copied file. Notice that the file icon moves with the mouse pointer. If you are copying more than one file, more than one file icon appears.

5. Release the mouse button. The File Manager displays the Confirm Mouse Operation dialog box.

6. Confirm that the file is being copied to the correct location, and then click **Yes**.

If you have problems...   If the Confirm Mouse Operation dialog box asks whether you want to move the file instead of copy it, you forgot to press and hold down **Ctrl**. To copy the file to a different directory on the same disk, you must press **Ctrl** before you drag the pointer.

Moving Files

You can easily move files from one location to another by dragging them from one directory window to another.

To move a file to a different disk, follow these steps:

1. In one window, open the directory that contains the file you want to move.

2. In another window, open the disk drive and the directory to which you want to move the file.

3. Select the file you want to move.

4. Press and hold down **Shift**, and drag the icon to the new location.

5. Release the mouse button. The Confirm Mouse Operation dialog box appears.

6. Confirm that the file is being moved to the correct location, and then click Yes.

If you have problems...	If the Confirm Mouse Operation dialog box asks whether you want to copy the file instead of moving it, you forgot to press and hold down **Shift**. To move a file to a different disk, you must press and hold down **Shift** before you drag the file.

To move a file to a different directory on the same disk, follow these steps:

1. In one window, open the directory that contains the file you want to move.

2. In another window, make sure that the directory to which you want to move the file is displayed.

3. Select the file that you want to move.

4. Drag the icon to the new location.

5. Release the mouse button. The Confirm Mouse Operation dialog box appears.

6. Confirm that the file is being moved to the correct location, and then click Yes.

Deleting Files

With the File Manager, you can delete a single file or a group of files. Because you see on-screen the files you are deleting, avoiding mistakes is easier.

To delete a file, follow these steps:

1. Open the directory that contains the file you want to delete.

2. Select the file.

3. Choose **F**ile, **D**elete. The Delete dialog box appears.

5

Confirm the file name and the current directory name to make sure that you are deleting the correct file.

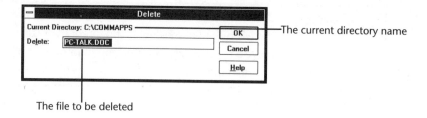

The current directory name

The file to be deleted

4. Click OK. The Confirm File Delete dialog box appears.

5. Confirm the file again, and then click **Yes**.

Note: *If you are deleting more than one file at a time and you are absolutely sure that all the files you have selected are correct, choose Yes to **A**ll in the Confirm File Delete dialog box. Then the File Manager will not prompt you to confirm each deletion.*

Renaming Files

To rename a file, follow these steps:

1. Open the directory that contains the file you want to rename.

2. Select the file you want to rename.

3. Choose File, Rename. The Rename dialog box appears, with the file name entered in the From text box.

Use the Rename dialog box to change the name of a selected file.

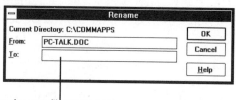

Type the new file name here

4. In the **T**o text box, type the new file name.

5. Click OK.

Working with Directories

In the File Manager, you easily can create, rename, move, or delete entire directories, as explained in the following sections.

Creating a Directory

To create a directory in the File Manager, follow these steps:

1. Open the directory in which you want to create the new directory.

2. Choose **F**ile, **C**reate Directory. The Create Directory dialog box appears.

In the Create Directory dialog box, type a name for the new directory.

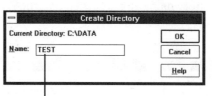

Type the new directory name here

3. In the **N**ame text box, type a name for the new directory.

4. Click OK.

The new directory appears in the directory tree and in the file list area as a directory within the current directory.

The new directory—

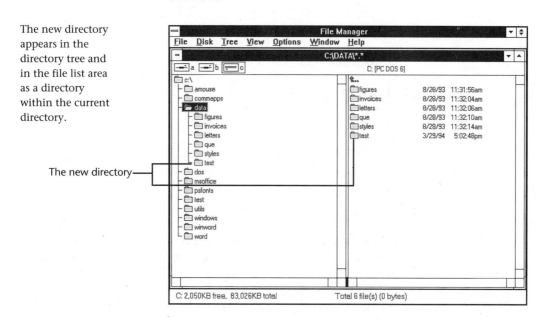

5

If you have problems... If Windows displays a warning message telling you that the directory already exists, you have tried to create a directory with the same name as an existing directory. Click OK, and use a different directory name, or make the new directory a subdirectory of a different directory.

Renaming a Directory

To rename a directory, follow these steps:

1. Select the directory you want to rename.

2. Choose **F**ile, Re**n**ame. The Rename dialog box appears, with the directory name already entered in the From text box.

The old directory name

You can easily rename an existing directory.

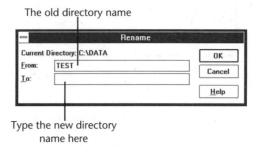

Type the new directory name here

3. In the **T**o text box, type the new directory name.

4. Click OK.

Moving a Directory

You can move a directory to a different disk, or you can make it a subdirectory of a different directory. When you move a directory, all the subdirectories and files it contains are moved with it.

To move a directory, follow these steps:

1. Select the directory you want to move.

2. Drag the directory to the new location. Notice that the folder icon moves with the mouse. The Confirm Mouse Operation dialog box appears.

3. Confirm that the directory is being moved to the correct location, and then click **Y**es.

Deleting Directories

When you delete a directory, all the subdirectories and files it contains are deleted as well.

To delete a directory, follow these steps:

1. Select the directory you want to delete.

2. Choose **F**ile, **D**elete. The Delete dialog box appears.

In the Delete dialog box, confirm that the directory specified in the De**l**ete text box is the one you want to delete.

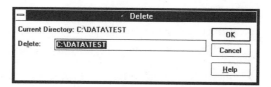

3. Click OK. The Confirm Directory Delete dialog box appears.

4. Confirm that the specified directory is the one you want to delete, and then choose **Y**es.

Note: *If the directory you are deleting contains files or subdirectories, Windows asks you to confirm each deletion. To delete all the files and subdirectories without confirmation, choose Yes to A**l**l in the Confirm Delete dialog box.*

Formatting Diskettes

Caution
Formatting wipes out all existing data. Use a blank diskette, or be sure you do not need the existing files on the diskette.

You can use the File Manager to format diskettes in either drive A or drive B.

To format diskettes, follow these steps:

1. Insert the diskette you want to format into the diskette drive.

2. Choose **D**isk, **F**ormat Disk. The Format Disk dialog box appears.

5

In the Format Disk dialog box, specify the capacity and location of the diskette you want to format.

Choose a diskette drive here

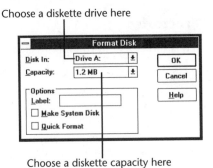

Choose a diskette capacity here

3. If necessary, click the drop-down arrow next to the **D**isk In text box to choose the diskette drive where the diskette is located.

4. If necessary, click the drop-down arrow next to the **C**apacity text box to choose the capacity of the diskette to be formatted.

5. Click OK. The Confirm Format Disk dialog box appears, reminding you that all existing data on the disk will be erased.

6. Click **Y**es to begin formatting the disk.

When the format is complete, you see a message asking whether you want to format another diskette. Click **Y**es to format another. Click **N**o to return to the File Manager window.

Copying a Diskette

You can use the File Manager to copy a diskette's contents to another diskette that is the same size and capacity. If you have two diskette drives of the same size, you can put the source diskette in one and the destination diskette in the other. If you have only one diskette drive or if you have two diskette drives of different sizes, you can use one diskette drive.

Note: *You can, of course, copy files and directories from one disk or diskette to another that is not the same size and capacity. However, to copy the entire diskette, both the source and the destination diskettes must be the same size and capacity.*

To copy a diskette, follow these steps:

1. Choose **D**isk, **C**opy Disk. The Copy Disk dialog box appears.

Choose the drive where the
source diskette is located here

You can copy the
information on a
diskette to a
diskette of the
same size and
capacity.

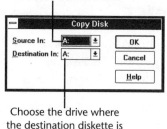

Choose the drive where
the destination diskette is
located here

2. If necessary, click the drop-down arrow next to the **S**ource In text box, and choose the drive into which you will insert the diskette you want to copy.

3. If necessary, click the drop-down arrow next to the **D**estination In text box, and choose the drive into which you will insert the blank diskette.

4. Click OK. The Confirm Copy Disk dialog box appears, reminding you that all the existing data on the destination disk will be erased by the copy procedure.

5. Click **Y**es. The Copy Disk dialog box appears, prompting you to insert the source diskette.

6. Insert the diskette you want to copy into the correct drive.

7. Click OK. The copy process begins.

At the appropriate time, the File Manager prompts you to insert the destination diskette into the correct drive and to click OK to continue. You may need to change diskettes more than once.

8. When the diskette is copied, the File Manager asks whether you want to copy another. Choose **Y**es to copy another diskette. Choose **N**o to return to the File Manager window.

5

Starting an Application Program from the File Manager

In Chapter 4, "Making Windows Work," you learned several ways to start application programs from the Program Manager. You can also start application programs directly from the File Manager.

Note: *Application programs are started using executable files. Executable files are usually identified by one of three file extensions: EXE, COM, or BAT. To determine the name of the executable file used to start a particular application program, consult the application program's document.*

To start an application program from the File Manager, follow these steps:

1. Open the directory that contains the program files for the application program you want to start.

2. Double-click the file that starts the application program. The program starts.

You can start an application program from the File Manager by double-clicking the file that runs the application program. Here, IBMAVD.EXE is the executable file used to start IBM AntiVirus for DOS.

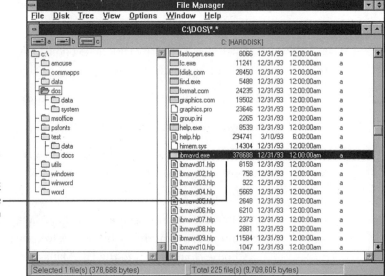

Double-click the EXE file to start the application program

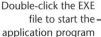

If you have problems...   If you do not know which file runs the application program, consult your application program documentation. Usually, application program files have EXE extensions. For example, the file PBRUSH.EXE starts and runs the Paintbrush program.

Changing the File Manager Font

Font
A specific size and style of character that can be printed or displayed on a computer.

If you want to change the appearance of the File Manager on-screen, you can change the *font* used to display characters.

To change the File Manager font, follow these steps:

1. Choose **O**ptions on the menu bar to show the Options menu.

2. Choose **F**ont from the Options menu. The Font dialog box appears.

In the Font dialog box, you can choose the font, font style, and font size you want displayed in the File Manager.

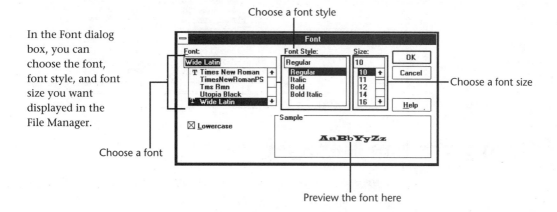

Choose a font style

Choose a font size

Choose a font

Preview the font here

3. In the **F**ont list, select the font you want to use. You can preview a sample of the font in the Sample area.

4. In the Font St**y**le list, select the font style you want to use.

5. In the **S**ize list, select the size font you want to use.

Note: *Fonts are measured in points; 72 points equal one inch. The larger the point size, the larger the font characters.*

6. To display both uppercase and lowercase characters, choose the **L**owercase check box so that it shows an x.

7. Choose OK. The File Manager display changes.

5

The File Manager font is 12-point boldface italic Arial shown here.

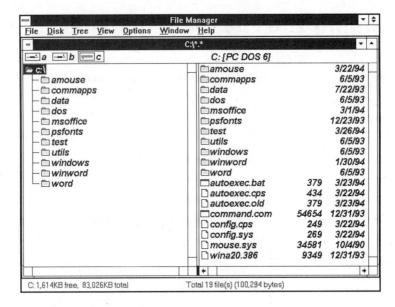

Closing the File Manager

You use the same methods to close the File Manager that you use to close any Windows application program.

To close the File Manager, double-click the Control menu button at the left end of the File Manager title bar.

If you have problems...

If you double-click the Control menu button but nothing happens, you are probably double-clicking the directory window Control menu button, not the File Manager Control menu button. Be sure to click the Control menu button at the left end of the File Manager title bar.

Part II
Beyond the Basics

Chapter 6

Customizing Your Desktop

In Windows, the Control Panel enables you to customize the way your mouse, keyboard, screen, and desktop work. When you change an option in the Control Panel, the change remains in effect until you change the setting again—even after you leave Windows.

In this chapter, you learn how to use the Control Panel to set the system date and time, customize the mouse, customize the keyboard, customize the desktop, and customize the screen.

Starting the Control Panel

The Control Panel is in the Program Manager's Main group. To start the Control Panel, double-click the Control Panel program icon.

The icons in the Control Panel window represent settings you can customize in Windows.

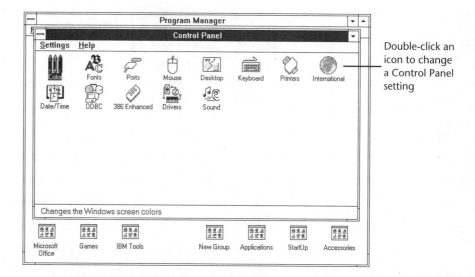

Double-click an icon to change a Control Panel setting

If you have problems... Your Control Panel may not have exactly the same icons as the ones shown in the illustrations for this chapter. You probably have additional icons if you have installed other devices, such as an extra pointing device, or if you are on a network.

Changing the System Date and Time

When you use your computer to create a file or save a document, PC DOS marks the file with the date and time you saved it or updated it. This information, displayed when you view a directory listing in the File Manager or from the PC DOS prompt, is helpful when you want to find the most recent version of a file or want to check when you typed a report.

You can change the date and time whenever you need to, such as if you change to daylight savings time or if you move to a new time zone.

To change your computer's system date and time, follow these steps:

1. Open the Control Panel window.

2. Double-click the Date/Time icon. The Date & Time dialog box appears.

Change the date here

In the Date & Time dialog box, you can change the system date and time.

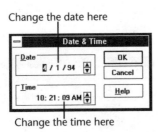

Change the time here

3. Click the part of the date or time that is incorrect. The insertion point moves to that spot.

4. Click the up- or down-arrow button to the right of the date or time until the setting is correct, or use the keyboard to type the correct number.

5. Repeat steps 3 and 4 to change other parts of the time and date.

6. Click OK when the date and time are correct.

Customizing the Mouse

You can control how fast the mouse pointer moves across the screen, how fast you need to double-click, and even which mouse button counts as the left button. You can also turn on the Mouse Trails feature, which traces the movements of the mouse pointer on-screen.

To customize the mouse settings, follow these steps:

1. Open the Control Panel window.

2. Double-click the Mouse icon. The Mouse dialog box appears.

Click here for faster tracking speed

You can customize the mouse settings to control the way the mouse responds.

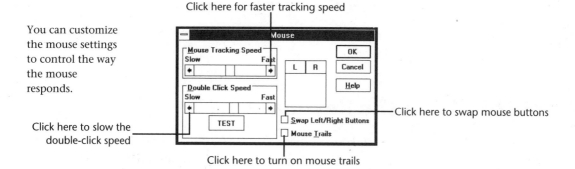

Click here to swap mouse buttons

Click here to slow the double-click speed

Click here to turn on mouse trails

3. In the **M**ouse Tracking Speed area, take one of the following steps:

■ Click the arrow under the word `Fast` to increase the speed with which the mouse pointer responds to mouse movements.

■ Click the arrow under the word `Slow` to decrease the speed with which the mouse pointer responds to mouse movements.

4. In the **D**ouble Click Speed area, take one of the following actions:

■ Click the arrow under the word `Fast` to increase the speed with which the mouse responds to a double-click. (This setting means that you must double-click faster for the mouse to respond.)

■ Click the arrow under the word `Slow` to decrease the speed with which the mouse responds to a double-click. (This setting means that you can double-click more slowly and still get a response.)

6

> **Note:** *You can test the double-click speed to see whether it is comfortable for you to use. Double-click the TEST box. If it turns darker, the mouse registered the double-click. If the TEST box does not turn darker, you are clicking too fast or too slow. Adjust the speed and try again.*

5. Click the check box next to **S**wap Left/Right buttons if you want to use the right mouse button to register left mouse button clicks, and the left mouse button to register right mouse button clicks. This option is particularly useful if you are left-handed and want to do most of your clicking with the index finger on your left hand.

6. Click the check box next to Mouse **T**rails if you want the mouse to leave a trail across the screen as it moves.

7. Choose OK to accept the settings and return to the Control Panel window.

Customizing the Keyboard

The Keyboard option enables you to control how fast a key repeats when you press and hold it down. In addition, you can specify how long your computer waits while you hold down a key before that key repeats.

To customize your keyboard, follow these steps:

1. Open the Control Panel window.

2. Double-click the Keyboard icon. The Keyboard dialog box appears.

Adjust the speed with which the keyboard responds to a repeated key press here

You can set and test your keyboard response time in the Keyboard dialog box.

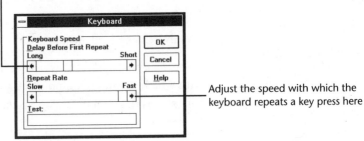

Adjust the speed with which the keyboard repeats a key press here

3. In the **D**elay Before First Repeat area, take one of the following actions:

- Click the arrow under the word `Short` to decrease the amount of time between the first response to a key press and a repeat of the action if you do not release the key.

- Click the arrow under the word `Long` to increase the amount of time between the first response to a key press and a repeat of the action if you do not release the key. This option gives you more time to release the key before the keyboard repeats the action.

4. In the **R**epeat Rate area, take one of the following actions:

- Click the arrow under the word `Fast` to increase the speed with which the keyboard repeats an action if you hold down the key.

- Click the arrow under the word `Slow` to decrease the speed with which the keyboard repeats an action if you hold down the key. This option gives you more time to release the key without repeating the action.

5. Click OK to accept the settings and return to the Control Panel window.

Note: *You can test the keyboard response rates by using the **T**est area in the Keyboard dialog box. Click within the **T**est box; then press and hold down any key. You can see how long it takes for the keyboard to register the key press and then how quickly (or slowly) the keyboard repeats the key press.*

Choosing a Color Scheme

By now, you have probably noticed that different elements in Windows appear in different colors. The title bar is one color, the menu bar another, selected text another, menu text still another, and so on. Windows gives you a wide variety of different color schemes from which you can choose to give your Windows programs the look you want.

To choose a pre-set color scheme, follow these steps:

1. Open the Control Panel window.

2. Double-click the Color icon. The Color dialog box appears.

The preview area

You can select
a pre-set color
scheme, or you
can create your
own using the
Color Palette.

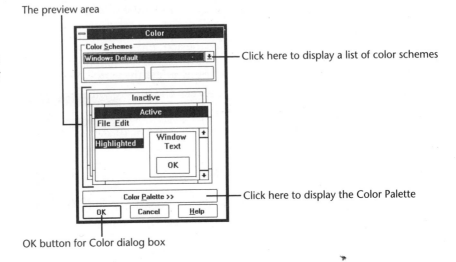

Click here to display a list of color schemes

Click here to display the Color Palette

OK button for Color dialog box

3. Click the arrow in the Color **S**chemes text box to drop down a list
of color schemes.

4. Click a color scheme from the list. The selected colors appear in the
preview area.

5. Choose OK to accept the selected color scheme.

If you have problems...	If you click OK and nothing happens, you may be clicking the OK button in the preview area. That button shows you only the color that buttons will appear in. The actual OK button for the Color dialog box is on the bottom line of the box.

Creating a Custom Color Scheme

You can pick and choose a certain color for each element of Windows,
giving your Windows programs a unique appearance. You can change an
existing color scheme or create a new color scheme by assigning new
colors to many parts of the Windows screen.

To create your own color scheme, follow the steps on the next page.

1. Open the Control Panel window.

2. Double-click the Color icon to display the Color dialog box.

3. Choose Color **P**alette from the Color dialog box.

You can customize
the Windows
colors by choosing
colors from the
Color Palette.

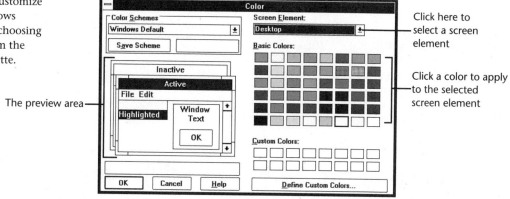

The preview area

Click here to
select a screen
element

Click a color to apply
to the selected
screen element

4. From the Color **S**chemes drop-down list, choose a color scheme to
use as a basis for the new color scheme.

**If you have
problems...**

Don't worry about altering an existing color scheme. You can save your
changes as a new scheme with a different name and avoid affecting the
existing color scheme.

6

5. Click the arrow next to the Screen **E**lement text box to drop down
a list of screen elements.

6. Select the part of the screen you want to change.

7. In the **B**asic Colors palette, click the color you want the screen
element to be. The preview area reflects your change.

8. Repeat steps 5 through 7 to change the colors of other screen
elements until you like the overall appearance of the screen in
the preview area.

9. Choose S**a**ve Scheme to save the new color scheme. The Save
Scheme dialog box appears.

In the Save
Scheme dialog
box, you can type
a name for your
color scheme.

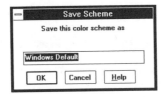

Caution
If you do not type
a new name, the
changes are made
to the current color
scheme.

10. In the text box of the Save Scheme dialog box, type a new name for the color scheme.

11. Choose OK in the Save Scheme dialog box.

12. Choose OK in the Color dialog box to return to the Control Panel window.

Changing the Desktop Background

Wallpaper
A drawing or
scanned picture
used for the desk-
top background.

One way to modify the appearance of Windows is to change the desktop background. You can add patterns and *wallpaper*, and you can turn on a screen saver to prolong the life of your display. To change the appearance of the desktop, use the Desktop dialog box.

To open the Desktop dialog box, follow these steps:

1. Open the Control Panel window.

2. Double-click the Desktop icon. The Desktop dialog box appears.

You can change
many aspects of
the Windows
desktop by
changing the
settings in the
Desktop dialog
box.

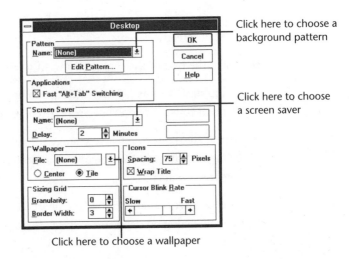

Click here to choose a
background pattern

Click here to choose
a screen saver

Click here to choose a wallpaper

Customizing the Desktop Pattern

To change the desktop pattern, follow these steps:

1. Double-click the Desktop icon in the Control Panel window to open the Desktop dialog box.

2. In the Pattern area, click the arrow next to the **N**ame text box to drop down a list of pattern names.

3. Select a pattern from the list.

4. Choose Edit **P**attern to view the pattern.

5. Choose OK to return to the Desktop dialog box.

6. Choose OK to return to the Control Panel.

Note: *To get a clear view of the new pattern, minimize the Program Manager so that the desktop appears without any windows open.*

The Desktop pattern has been changed to Quilt.

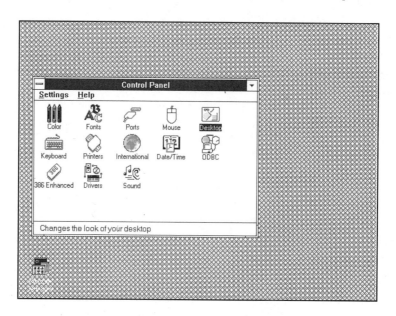

6

If you have problems...   Using a pattern requires a great deal of system memory. If you add a pattern and your system runs very slowly, change the Desktop pattern back to None.

Customizing the Wallpaper

Instead of using a pattern for the desktop, you can use a drawing or scanned picture—called wallpaper—for your background. Windows includes several wallpapers you can use, or you can create your own.

If you have problems...   Using wallpaper requires a great deal of system memory. If you add wallpaper and your system runs very slowly, change the Wallpaper option back to None.

To customize the Desktop wallpaper, follow these steps:

1. Double-click the Desktop icon in the Control Panel window to open the Desktop dialog box.

2. In the Wallpaper area, click the arrow next to the **F**ile text box to drop down a list of available wallpapers.

If you have problems...   If no files appear in the Wallpaper list, you have no files with BMP extensions in the Windows directory. You can reinstall Windows to replace the BMP files.

---

3. Select a file from the list.

4. Select the **T**ile option to apply the wallpaper evenly across the desktop. Choose the **C**enter option to display one graphic image in the center of your screen.

5. Choose OK to close the Desktop dialog box. The wallpaper appears on the desktop.

The ARCADE.BMP file is used to wallpaper the desktop.

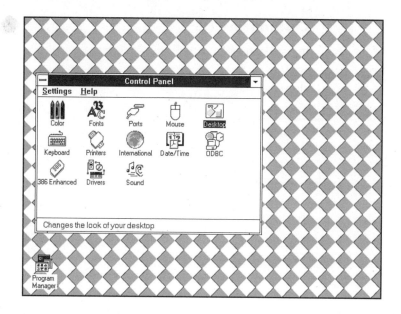

Using a Screen Saver

Screen saver
A program that displays a changing image on your display to reduce the possibility of image burn-in.

If you leave Windows on for a very long time, sooner or later it may burn a faint image on your display screen. You will see the image even when the display is turned off or when you are working from the PC DOS prompt. To avoid this problem, you can turn off Windows when you are not using it, or you can use a *screen saver*.

To turn on a Windows screen saver, follow these steps:

1. Double-click the Desktop icon from the Control Panel to open the Desktop dialog box.

2. In the Screen Saver area, click the arrow next to the **N**ame box to drop down the list of available screen savers.

3. Choose a screen saver from the list.

4. In the **D**elay text box, enter the length of time you want the computer to remain idle before Windows starts the screen saver.

5. Choose T**e**st to view the screen saver. To end the test, move the mouse.

6. Choose OK.

6

Chapter 7

Working with the Text Editor

ASCII file

A file that contains alphanumeric and control characters, such as text. AUTOEXEC.BAT is an example of an ASCII file.

PC DOS comes with the E Editor, a full-screen text editor that enables you to create, edit, and print memos, letters, and *ASCII files*, quickly and easily.

This chapter introduces you to the E Editor. You learn the basics of starting the E Editor and of using it to create, modify, and print a text file.

Starting the E Editor

You can start the E Editor from the PC DOS command line, from a shell program such as the IBM DOS Shell, or from Windows. The file used to start the E Editor is E.EXE.

To start the E Editor from Windows, follow these steps:

1. Choose **F**ile, **R**un in the Program Manager window. The Run dialog box appears.

One way to start the E Editor is from the Windows Program Manager.

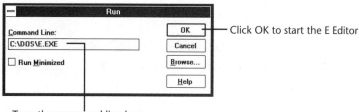

Click OK to start the E Editor

Type the command line here

2. In the Command Line text box, type the file specification for the E.EXE file. For example, type **C:\DOS\E.EXE**.

3. Click OK. The E Editor starts, and a full-screen window opens.

To start the E Editor from the File Manager, open the DOS directory folder and double-click the E.EXE file in the file list area. Or you can add a program item for the E Editor to the IBM Tools program group and then start the E Editor from that group. For information on starting programs and adding items to a program group, see chapter 4, "Making Windows Work."

Understanding the E Editor

The E Editor creates and saves unformatted, or ASCII, text files. ASCII files contain only text characters and a few control characters you can enter on your keyboard, such as tabs and returns.

Cursor
A marker indicating where text will appear when you type.

The E Editor provides a full-screen window for entering text. Characters that you type on your keyboard appear at the *cursor* location, between the Top of file and Bottom of file markers.

If you do not open an existing file, the E Editor starts with a blank, unnamed file open in a full-screen window.

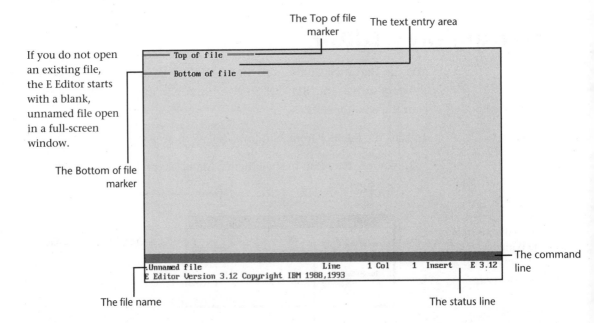

The Top of file marker   The text entry area

The Bottom of file marker

The file name

The status line

The command line

The *E Editor status line* near the bottom of the screen indicates the file name as well as the text line number, the column number, and whether Insert mode is turned on.

E Editor command line
An area in the E Editor window where you can enter text-editing commands.

The line above the status line is the *E Editor command line*. You can use the command line to perform E Editor commands such as naming a file.

When you begin typing text, the actions associated with the *function keys* are displayed in the function key area, below the status line.

Function keys
Special command keys on your keyboard that have the letter *F* followed by a number.

The function keys enable you to perform most E Editor tasks with only one keystroke. You can press the Alt, Shift, or Scroll key to display additional function keys. Table 7.1 lists the basic E Editor function keys and their associated actions.

Table 7.1 E Editor Function Keys	
Key	**Action**
F1	Displays on-line Help.
F2	Saves the text file you are editing without closing the file.
F3	Exits the E Editor and returns to the IBM DOS Shell without saving the file. If changes have been made since the last save, the E Editor asks if you want to exit without saving. From the on-line Help, F3 returns to the E Editor.
F4	Saves the current file and exits the E Editor.
F6	Shows the options for drawing text graphics.
F7	Changes the current file name.
F8	Opens the specified file for editing without closing the current file.
F9	Cancels editing changes made to the current line.
F10	Displays the next open file for editing without closing the current file.

7

Creating a Text File

Word wrap
The way text automatically moves down to the beginning of the next line when the current line is filled.

To create a text file, just type your text in the E Editor window. E Editor does not have *word wrap*, so you must press **Enter** to move the cursor to the next line. You can type up to 254 characters plus a carriage return on each line in the E Editor.

Note: *You can set margins in the E Editor to simulate word wrap.*

If you have problems...

If you do not press Enter when your text reaches the edge of the screen, the line continues to scroll to the right, and the characters at the beginning of the line disappear off the left side of the screen. Press the left-arrow key to scroll back to the beginning of the line, or press **Home**.

You can use the cursor control keys to move within the file as you type or to view parts of the file that have already been entered. Table 7.2 lists the cursor control keys and their functions.

Table 7.2 E Editor Cursor Control Keys

Key	Action
Up arrow	Moves up one line.
Down arrow	Moves down one line.
Left arrow	Moves left one character.
Right arrow	Moves right one character.
Home	Moves to column 1 of the current line.
End	Moves to the last character of the current line.
PgUp	Moves up one page of text.
PgDn	Moves down one page of text.
Ctrl+Home	Moves to the first line in the file.
Ctrl+End	Moves to the last line in the file.
Ctrl+PgUp	Moves to the first line of the current screen.
Ctrl+PgDn	Moves to the last line of the current screen.
Ctrl+left arrow	Moves to the first character of the word on which the cursor is currently positioned.
Ctrl+right arrow	Moves to the last character of the word on which the cursor is currently positioned.
Ctrl+Enter	Moves to column 1 of the next line.
Tab	Moves to the next tab stop.
Shift+Tab	Moves to the previous tab stop.
Esc	Toggles to and from the E Editor command line.

Editing with the E Editor

The PC DOS E Editor is a powerful line editor that contains many of the same features found in high-end word processors. With just one or two keystrokes, you can perform most editing tasks, including inserting, deleting, moving, and copying blocks of text.

Entering Text in a File

When you open a new file in the E Editor, you can begin typing your new document. If you open an existing file, you can immediately make changes.

The E Editor is a line editor, which means you must manually insert line breaks, or line feeds, as you type.

To insert a line break, simply press **Enter** at the point where you want to end the current line and start a new line. The cursor moves to the beginning of the next line.

In the E Editor, you must manually insert line breaks by pressing Enter.

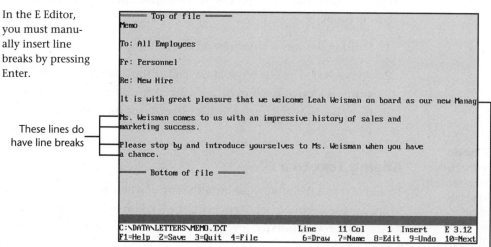

These lines do have line breaks

This line doesn't have a line break, so the text continues beyond the edge of the screen

If you try later to insert a line break in an existing line of text by pressing Enter, you will see that a new line is inserted between the current line of text and the next line; the original line of text remains intact. Furthermore, you cannot remove a line feed by pressing Backspace or Delete.

If you did not insert a line break when you first typed a line of text, you can go back and split the line.

To split an existing line of text into two separate lines, follow these steps:

1. Position the cursor on the character you want as the first character of the new line.

2. Press **Alt+S**. A new line is inserted in the file, and the text from the cursor location to the end of the line is moved to the beginning of the new line. The cursor remains in its previous position, which is now the end of the original line.

If you have problems...   If the new line begins with a space, you had the cursor positioned on a space between two words. Be sure to position the cursor on the character you want to begin the new line before you press **Alt+S**.

To remove a line break and join two consecutive lines into one line, follow these steps:

1. Position the cursor anywhere on the first line.

2. Press **Alt+J**. The line break at the end of the line on which the cursor is located is removed, automatically joining the two lines into one. Now the line probably extends past the edge of the viewing area.

Insert mode
A setting that tells the E Editor to insert new text at the cursor location, pushing existing text to the right.

Replace mode
A setting that tells the E Editor to replace, or overwrite, existing text as you type.

Adding Text to a File

To add text to a file, simply position the cursor where you want the text to appear and begin typing. By default, the E Editor opens in *Insert mode*. As you type, text is inserted into the file at the cursor location.

If you want to overwrite existing text, change to *Replace mode* by pressing the Insert key on your keyboard. Text that you type replaces existing text at the cursor location.

E Editor has two ways of indicating the mode in which it is currently working.

■ The status line. The word `Insert` indicates Insert mode. The word `Replace` indicates Replace mode.

■ The cursor. A rectangular cursor indicates Insert mode. An underline indicates Replace mode.

If the word `Insert` appears on the status line and the cursor is a rectangular shape, the E Editor is in Insert mode.

```
======= Top of file =======
Memo

To: All Employees

Fr: Personnel

Re: New Hire

It is with great pleasure that we welcome Leah Weisman on board as our new Manag

Ms. Weisman comes to us with an impressive history of sales and
marketing success.

Please stop by and introduce yourselves to Ms. Weisman when you have
a chance.
======= Bottom of file =======




C:\DATA\LETTERS\MEMO.TXT              Line    15 Col    10  Insert    E 3.12
F1=Help  2=Save  3=Quit  4=File              6=Draw  7=Name  8=Edit  9=Undo  10=Next
```

The word `Insert`

If the word `Replace` appears on the status line and the cursor is an underline, the E Editor is in Replace mode.

```
======= Top of file =======
Memo

To: All Employees

Fr: Personnel

Re: New Hire

It is with great pleasure that we welcome Leah Weisman on board as our new Manag

Ms. Weisman comes to us with an impressive history of sales and
marketing success.

Please stop by and introduce yourselves to Ms. Weisman when you have
a chance.
======= Bottom of file =======




C:\DATA\LETTERS\MEMO.TXT              Line    15 Col    10  Replace   E 3.12
F1=Help  2=Save  3=Quit  4=File              6=Draw  7=Name  8=Edit  9=Undo  10=Next
```

The word `Replace`

7

Deleting Text from a File

With the E Editor, you can remove text one character at a time, one word at a time, or one line at a time.

To remove text one character at a time, take one of the following actions:

- Press **Delete** to remove the character on which the cursor is currently located.

- Press **Backspace** to remove the character to the left of the cursor.

To remove text one word at a time, follow these steps:

1. Position the cursor at the beginning of the word you want to delete.

2. Press **Ctrl+D**. The characters from the cursor to the end of the word are deleted.

To remove an entire line of text, follow these steps:

1. Position the cursor anywhere on the line you want to delete.

2. Press **Ctrl+Backspace**. The entire line is deleted, and the text below the deleted line moves up one line.

Marking Text

Mark
To select text in a file.

With the E Editor, you can manipulate the contents of a file by *marking* the text. After you mark the text, you can perform such functions as copying, moving, or deleting.

In a single line, you can mark any amount of text from a single character to the entire line. You can also mark several lines, a rectangular block, or the entire file. No matter how much text is marked, the marked area appears highlighted on-screen.

To mark a single character, or a series of characters not in a block or a line, follow these steps:

1. Position the cursor on the character you want to mark.

2. Press **Alt+Z**.

To mark a word, follow these steps:

1. Position the cursor anywhere within the word you want to mark.

2. Press **Alt+W**.

Note: *If the cursor is positioned on a space when you press Alt+W, the E Editor marks the next word to the right of the cursor. If there is no word to the right, it marks the next word to the left of the cursor. If there are no words at all on the current line, the E Editor marks the current space character.*

To mark an entire line, follow these steps:

1. Position the cursor anywhere within the line you want to mark.

2. Press **Alt+L**.

To mark a block of text, follow these steps:

1. Position the cursor anywhere within the first line you want to mark.

2. Press **Alt+ L**.

3. Move the cursor to the last line of text that you want to mark.

4. Press **Alt + L**.

The E Editor marks the first and last lines and all the lines between them.

To mark a rectangular block of text, follow these steps:

1. Position the cursor on the character that will be in the upper left corner of the rectangular block.

2. Press **Alt+B**.

3. Position the cursor on the character that will be in the lower right corner of the rectangular block.

4. Press **Alt+B** again.

Note: *Marking rectangular blocks of text is particularly useful when you are working with columns of data. It is important to note, however, that when you copy or move a rectangular block of data, you must place the block into blank space, or it will overwrite any existing data.*

7

A rectangular block of text has been marked and is highlighted on-screen.

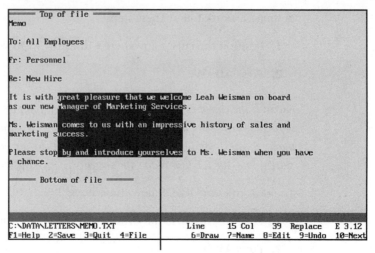

```
══════ Top of file ══════
Memo

To: All Employees

Fr: Personnel

Re: New Hire

It is with great pleasure that we welcome Leah Weisman on board
as our new Manager of Marketing Services.

Ms. Weisman comes to us with an impressive history of sales and
marketing success.

Please stop by and introduce yourselves to Ms. Weisman when you have
a chance.
══════ Bottom of file ══════



C:\DATA\LETTERS\MEMO.TXT            Line    15 Col    39  Replace    E 3.12
F1=Help  2=Save   3=Quit   4=File          6=Draw  7=Name  8=Edit  9=Undo  10=Next
```

Marked block of text

To unmark any text, press **Alt+U**. To delete marked text, press **Alt+D**.

Copying Text

Copy

To place an exact copy of marked text at a different location.

You can *copy* marked text to a new location in the same file or in another file, without affecting the original text.

To copy text, follow these steps:

1. Open the file that contains the text you want to copy.

2. Mark the text you want to copy.

3. If you want to copy the text to another file, press **F8** and type the path and file name of the other file without closing the original file.

4. Position the cursor at the location where you want to insert the copied text. If you need to switch from one open file to the other, press **F10** to switch.

5. Press **Alt+C** to copy the text.

Note: *The E Editor stores marked text in a temporary storage area. Until you mark different text, you can press Alt+C as many times as you want to insert the text into several locations.*

Moving Text

Move
To move the original text from the document and place an exact copy of the marked text at a different location.

You can *move* marked text from one location in a file to another location or from one file to another.

To move marked text, follow these steps:

1. Open the file that contains the text you want to move.

2. Mark the text you want to move.

3. If you want to move the text to a different file, press **F8** and type the path and file name of the file without closing the original file.

4. Position the cursor at the location where you want to insert the text. If you want to switch from one open file to the other, press **F10**.

5. Press **Alt+M**. The E Editor moves the text from its original location to the current cursor location. The existing text moves to allow for the insertion.

Naming and Saving a File with the E Editor

Before you can save a file with the E Editor, the file must have a name.

Note: *You can name a file at any time.*

To name and save a file, follow these steps:

1. Press **F7**, the Name function key. The cursor moves down to the E Editor command line. You enter the Name command there.

2. Type the file name. Remember to include the complete path. If you do not include the complete path, the file will be saved in the current directory.

3. Press **Enter**. The name appears under the command line.

4. Press **F4** to save the file and exit the E Editor.

7

Press F7 and enter
the complete path
and file name
on the E Editor
command line. In
this example, the
file MEMO.TXT
is stored in the
\DATA\LETTERS
subdirectory.

The command line

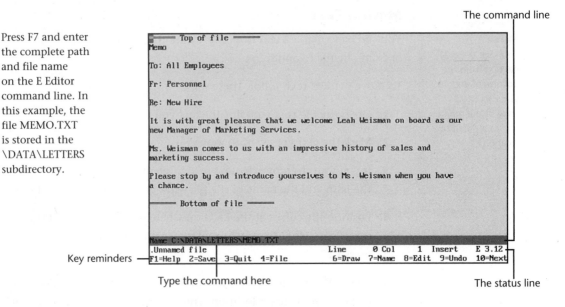

Key reminders

Type the command here

The status line

When you press
Enter, the path
and file name
appear on the
status line. Press
Esc to move the
cursor back to the
text area if you
want to continue
working with the
file.

You can view
the path and
file name here

You can also use the F7 function key to save a new version of the current
file with a new name. Renaming the current file doesn't change the
name of the previous version of the file already stored on your disk.
To rename an existing file, follow the same procedure used for naming a
new file. Press **Esc** to return to the text area, and continue editing the file
with its new name.

Saving a File

When you have completed entering or editing text, you must save the file. Actually, you should save the file periodically, even while you are still working on it. If something happens to disrupt your computer session, you will still have a fairly recent version of the file saved.

Note: *The E Editor has an Autosave feature that automatically saves the file you are working in at regular intervals, based on the number of times you press Enter. To activate Autosave, press* **Esc** *to move to the Command line. Type* **AUTOSAVE**, *press the* **spacebar**, *and then type a number indicating how many times you want to press Enter before the file is saved. For example, if you type AUTOSAVE 10, the E Editor will save your file after you press Enter ten times.*

The E Editor has two ways to save a file.

- You can save the file periodically and continue editing (F2).

- You can save the file and exit the E Editor (F4).

No matter which method of saving that you use, notice that when you begin to save the file, a message appears briefly in the function key area, telling you that the file is being saved.

To save the file and continue editing, press **F2**. The file is saved in the current directory or in the directory specified with the file name. You can continue editing the file.

To save the file and exit the E Editor, press **F4**. The file is saved with its current name and path, and you are returned to Windows.

You also can save the file with a new name or in a new directory. Type **SAVE** and the new path and file name. The file will be saved in the new directory or with the new name.

7

If you have problems...

If a `File not found` error message is displayed in the function key reminder area when you try to save a file, the file does not yet have a name. A file must have a name before it can be saved. Press **F7** to name the file, and then try saving it again.

Printing a File

You can use the E Editor to print the open file displayed on-screen. Before trying to print a file, make sure that your printer is turned on, that it is loaded with paper, and that it is correctly attached to your computer.

To print a file with the E Editor, follow these steps:

1. Start the E Editor, and open the file you want to print.

2. Press **Esc** to move the cursor to the E Editor command line.

3. Type **PRINT**, and press **Enter**. The E Editor prints the file.

Note: *You can print only a marked portion of a file. Simply mark the text you want to print, press **Esc** and type **PRINT** on the command line. When you press Enter, the E Editor prints only the marked text.*

The E Editor checks the printer before it prints.

If you have problems...   If the printer is not turned on, is out of paper, or is off-line, the E Editor displays the error message `Printer not ready`. Check your printer, and issue the PRINT command again.

Exiting the E Editor

When you have finished creating or editing text files, you can exit the E Editor and return to Windows. You can exit in one of two ways:

■ Press **F3** to exit. If you have made changes to any open file since the last time you saved it, the E Editor displays a message in the function key area, asking if you want to exit without saving. Press **Y** to return to Windows without saving the changes. Press **N** to return to the current file.

■ Press **F4** if you have more than one file open. The E Editor saves each open file in turn. When all files are closed, you are returned to Windows.

Chapter 8

Configuring Your Personal Computer

You can configure your computer so that PC DOS, your hardware, and your application programs work the way you need them to in your particular computing environment. This procedure can be as simple as customizing the appearance of the PC DOS command prompt or as complex as setting up a new hardware component.

Memory
The electronic circuitry where the computer stores information.

In addition, you can optimize the way your computer uses available *memory*. By allocating memory resources, you can be sure that your software and hardware run the way you need them to run.

In this chapter, you learn how to use the CONFIG.SYS and AUTOEXEC.BAT files to configure your computer and how to use RAMBoost to make as much memory as possible available for use.

Before you begin to examine and work with the CONFIG.SYS and AUTOEXEC.BAT files and with RAMBoost, you need to understand your computer's memory.

Understanding Memory

On your computer, memory provides temporary storage for programs and data. Your computer has two types of memory: read-only memory (ROM) and random-access memory (RAM).

ROM

Read-only memory that cannot be erased or added to. ROM provides the instructions the computer and PC DOS need to get started.

RAM

Random-access memory, the electronic memory that the computer uses to store information until it is needed or is stored on disk.

Address space

The amount of RAM available for use.

Real mode

The usual mode of operation, where all processors run as fast as 8086-based computers.

Conventional memory

The first 640K of memory installed on every computer. It is used for running the operating system and application programs and for storing data.

ROM is memory that you cannot erase or write on. ROM provides the instructions that the computer needs to get started each time you turn it on. The amount of ROM is determined by the hardware manufacturer. You cannot add more ROM.

RAM is like a blackboard; data is constantly being written, erased, and written again in RAM. Computers come with different amounts of RAM, and you can add more RAM.

RAM is contained on the main system board of your computer or on add-in memory boards. All programs must be loaded into RAM to run. In general, the more RAM you have, the more programs you can run, the more data you can work with at one time, and the faster your computer processes instructions.

Computers that are based on 80286 or higher processors and run the PC DOS operating system have a 1,024K (1 megabyte) *address space* when operating in *real mode*. This figure means that potentially 1M of memory is available.

However, no matter which processor your computer uses or how much memory you have installed, all information is processed in the first 640K—called *conventional memory*. The memory above 640K is reserved for use by devices and other system components.

Many programs have too many instructions to fit into 640K at one time. Waiting for the instructions to be swapped back and forth from a disk to memory is not practical, so computer technicians designed a method to enable your computer to use memory beyond the 640K limit for temporarily storing information.

The types of memory used by computers fall into five different categories:

- Conventional memory

- Upper (or reserved) memory

- High memory

- Extended memory

- Expanded memory

Conventional PC DOS Memory

The first 640K of memory installed on your computer is called conventional PC DOS memory. This is the memory that PC DOS uses to process application programs.

Upper (Reserved) Memory

Memory between 640K and 1M is known as the Upper Memory Block (UMB) and is reserved for use by video adapters, network hardware, ROM BIOS, and other hardware that uses computer memory. This memory, however, is never completely used. Some is always left over and can be used for loading TSRs, PC DOS tables, and network software. These Upper Memory Blocks are used by RAMBoost to free conventional PC DOS memory.

High Memory Area

The high memory area is the first 64K of extended memory located just above 1M. Some PC DOS programs running on 80286-based or higher computers can store portions of their operating code software in high memory.

Extended Memory (XMS)

Extended memory is all memory over 1M. Because extended memory cannot be accessed when the processor is in real mode, standard programs running under PC DOS cannot use extended memory.

Protected mode
A special mode of operation that 80286-based or higher computers can use to access extended memory.

On 80286-based and higher machines, some programs, such as RAM disks and disk-caching programs, automatically switch the processor to *protected mode* so that they can access this space. Extended memory can never be used on 8088-based and 8086-based machines because these processors do not support protected mode or memory above 1M.

Expanded Memory (EMS)

Expanded memory is a combination of hardware and software that uses a 64K area of memory, typically in the address space between 640K and 1,024K. Application programs must be written specifically to switch blocks of memory in and out of this window. The programs themselves use conventional memory to function and access this expanded memory only to store data.

8

Understanding CONFIG.SYS and AUTOEXEC.BAT

Most of your system's configuration information is stored in the two files that PC DOS runs each time you start your computer:

- *CONFIG.SYS*. A file created during installation of PC DOS and stored in the root directory. CONFIG.SYS contains special commands used by PC DOS to control the way the computer, the application programs, and the peripheral devices work. The commands in the CONFIG.SYS set up parameters for your computer's hardware components (such as memory boards, keyboard, mouse, and printer) so that PC DOS and application programs can use them. When PC DOS starts, it processes the commands in the CONFIG.SYS file.

Batch file

A file that contains a series of commands that PC DOS carries out sequentially.

- *AUTOEXEC.BAT*. A special *batch file* created during installation of PC DOS and stored in the root directory. AUTOEXEC.BAT contains a series of commands that PC DOS carries out sequentially immediately after executing the commands in the CONFIG.SYS file. AUTOEXEC.BAT can contain any commands you want to carry out when you start your system. For example, this file can contain commands that define the port to which your printer is connected, clear your screen of start-up messages, or start your favorite application program.

When you install PC DOS, Setup creates a basic system configuration that works for most people. The settings in your CONFIG.SYS file control the basic components of your system, such as memory and disk drives.

You can change your configuration at any time. If, however, you change your CONFIG.SYS file and the new settings are incorrect, your system will not start correctly.

If you have problems...

If you cannot start your computer after you have modified your CONFIG.SYS file, restart your computer using your start-up diskette (Diskette 1 of the PC DOS Setup diskettes), or bypass CONFIG.SYS and AUTOEXEC.BAT commands by using the procedure explained in the following section.

Bypassing CONFIG.SYS and AUTOEXEC.BAT Commands

If necessary, you can start your system without running all or part of your CONFIG.SYS and AUTOEXEC.BAT files. Bypassing these commands is useful if you are experiencing system problems that are related to the settings in your CONFIG.SYS file or AUTOEXEC.BAT file.

You can bypass start-up commands in either of two ways:

- You can bypass your start-up files completely.

- You can have PC DOS confirm each CONFIG.SYS and AUTOEXEC.BAT command when you start your computer.

Bypassing Your Start-Up Files Completely

If you are having system problems that are related to the commands in your CONFIG.SYS or AUTOEXEC.BAT files, you can temporarily bypass those files to start your computer. Then you can make changes to the files to fix the problems.

To bypass the start-up files, follow these steps:

1. Start your computer. Your computer runs through its start-up routine and looks for the PC DOS files. Then the computer displays the message `Starting PC DOS....`

2. Press **F5** as soon as the `Starting PC DOS...` message appears. PC DOS skips the CONFIG.SYS and AUTOEXEC.BAT files and loads using a temporary default configuration. The PC DOS command prompt appears on-screen.

If you have problems... Don't worry if your computer does not seem to be working the way it usually does. When you bypass the AUTOEXEC.BAT and CONFIG.SYS files completely, many components of your computer do not work. For example, any device that requires a software program called an installable device driver does not work because the installable device drivers are loaded by the commands in the CONFIG.SYS and AUTOEXEC.BAT files. (For more information on software device drivers, see the section "Configuring Device Drivers," later in this chapter.)

8

Confirming Each CONFIG.SYS
and AUTOEXEC.BAT Statement

Statement
A single command
line in a file.

You can have PC DOS prompt you for confirmation before running each *statement* in your CONFIG.SYS and AUTOEXEC.BAT files. This technique is useful if you want to test the commands as they start.

To set PC DOS to request confirmation before carrying out each CONFIG.SYS and AUTOEXEC.BAT command, follow these steps:

1. Start your computer. Your computer runs through its start-up routine and looks for the PC DOS files. Then the computer displays the message Starting PC DOS....

2. Press **F8** as soon as the Starting PC DOS... message appears. PC DOS displays each command in your CONFIG.SYS file, pausing to wait for confirmation.

3. To run the command, press **Y**. To skip the command, press **N**.

4. When PC DOS finishes processing the CONFIG.SYS file, it displays the following prompt:

   Process AUTOEXEC.BAT [Y,N]?

5. To confirm each statement in your AUTOEXEC.BAT file, press **Y**. To bypass your AUTOEXEC.BAT file completely, press **N**.

Viewing and Editing Your CONFIG.SYS File

You can easily view the contents of your CONFIG.SYS file by using the PC DOS TYPE command.

To display your CONFIG.SYS file on-screen, follow these steps:

1. At the PC DOS command prompt, type

   TYPE CONFIG.SYS

2. Press **Enter**. PC DOS displays your CONFIG.SYS file on-screen.

Note: *If the file takes up more than one screen, you may need to use the MORE command. At the PC DOS command prompt, type* **TYPE CONFIG.SYS ¦ MORE**, *and then press* **Enter**.

Enter the TYPE command here

You can view your
CONFIG.SYS file
without affecting
it by using the PC
DOS TYPE
command.

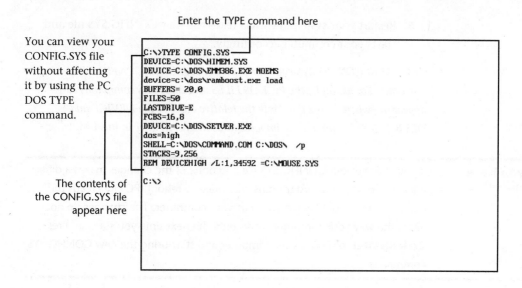

```
C:\>TYPE CONFIG.SYS
DEVICE=C:\DOS\HIMEM.SYS
DEVICE=C:\DOS\EMM386.EXE NOEMS
device=c:\dos\ramboost.exe load
BUFFERS= 20,0
FILES=50
LASTDRIVE=E
FCBS=16,8
DEVICE=C:\DOS\SETVER.EXE
dos=high
SHELL=C:\DOS\COMMAND.COM C:\DOS\ /p
STACKS=9,256
REM DEVICEHIGH /L:1,34592 =C:\MOUSE.SYS

C:\>
```

The contents of
the CONFIG.SYS file
appear here

You edit the CONFIG.SYS file by using a text editor, such as the E Editor, that can save files as unformatted (ASCII) text. Do not edit the CONFIG.SYS file using a word processing program that saves files in a document format. If you do, PC DOS will not be able to read the file, and your computer will not start. If you have a word processing program that can save files in ASCII format, you can use it to edit CONFIG.SYS. For information on using the E Editor, see Chapter 7, "Working with the Text Editor."

To edit your CONFIG.SYS file, follow these steps:

1. Make a copy of your CONFIG.SYS file on a separate diskette or on your hard disk. Name the copied file with a different extension, such as CONFIG.BAK. If something goes wrong with the edits, you can use the COPY command to copy the original file back into your root directory.

2. Open the CONFIG.SYS file using the E Editor.

3. Add or change CONFIG.SYS commands as necessary. For information about specific statements or commands, see the following sections.

   Note: *Each CONFIG.SYS command must begin on a separate line.*

4. When you have finished editing the CONFIG.SYS file, save your changes, and exit from the E Editor.

8

5. Restart your system. PC DOS reads the new CONFIG.SYS file and starts your computer accordingly.

Note: *Most CONFIG.SYS commands can appear in the CONFIG.SYS file in any order. For example, the PC DOS FILES and BUFFERS commands can appear anywhere in the file. Only the relative order of the DEVICE and DEVICEHIGH commands is important, as discussed later in this chapter.*

If you have problems...

If you change your CONFIG.SYS file and none of the changes makes a difference in the way your system runs, you need to reboot. PC DOS reads the CONFIG.SYS file only when you start your computer. The changes do not affect the way your computer works until the next time you start up. Press **Ctrl+Alt+Del** to reboot your computer and start using the new CONFIG.SYS commands.

Configuring Device Drivers

Device

A hardware peripheral attached to your computer and controlled by PC DOS.

Each hardware component of your computer is called a *device*. The keyboard, mouse, display, printer, disk drives, and memory boards are all devices. Each device has its own characteristics that can be customized.

PC DOS controls devices through *device drivers*.

Device driver

A special program file that provides instructions for controlling a hardware device.

PC DOS has built-in device drivers for the keyboard, display, hard and diskette drives, and communication ports. PC DOS adds these device drivers to your CONFIG.SYS file during installation. Other devices—such as memory boards, a mouse, or CD-ROM—have device drivers that are not built into PC DOS. The device drivers for these devices are called installable because you install them by adding commands to your CONFIG.SYS.

Installable device driver

A program file that controls certain hardware devices installed on a computer by adding commands to the CONFIG.SYS file.

To use an *installable device driver*, you must add a DEVICE command for that driver to your CONFIG.SYS file. The DEVICE command tells PC DOS what path to search to find the device driver file.

Many devices come with installation programs that automatically add the correct command to your CONFIG.SYS file. Before you install a new device, read the instruction manual carefully, and follow the directions.

When you add a device driver to your CONFIG.SYS file manually, you must type the DEVICE command statement into the CONFIG.SYS file using the correct PC DOS command syntax, just as you would type a command on the PC DOS command line. For more information on typing PC DOS commands, see Chapter 1, "Understanding System Basics," and Appendix A, "The PC DOS Top Twenty."

To add a device driver to your CONFIG.SYS file, follow these steps:

1. Open the CONFIG.SYS file, using the E Editor.

2. On a separate line, type

   DEVICE=*drive\path\device driver filename*

   (You can use either uppercase or lowercase letters.) For example, to load the HIMEM.SYS device driver from the C:\DOS directory, you type

   DEVICE=C:\DOS\HIMEM.SYS

When PC DOS reads this command, it loads the HIMEM.SYS device driver into memory. The HIMEM.SYS device driver remains in memory and manages extended memory.

Order of Commands in CONFIG.SYS

The order in which most commands appear in the CONFIG.SYS file does not matter. But the order is important for the DEVICE and DEVICEHIGH commands. (DEVICEHIGH loads drivers into upper memory.) Some device drivers must be in place for other device drivers to work.

When adding DEVICE drivers to your CONFIG.SYS file, make sure that they appear in the following order:

- HIMEM.SYS if your system has extended memory.

- Your expanded-memory manager if your system has an expanded-memory board.

- EMM386.EXE if your system is an 80386 or higher processor with extended memory.

  Note: *If your CONFIG.SYS file includes both an expanded-memory manager and EMM386, the EMM386 command line should include the NOEMS switch.*

8

- DPMS.EXE (DOS Protect Mode Services)

- Any other device drivers.

Note: *This list is intended to show the correct order for device drivers, not the specific commands your CONFIG.SYS file should contain. The contents of your system's CONFIG.SYS file depend on the type of system, the amount or type of memory, the hardware configuration, and the application programs you use.*

Sample CONFIG.SYS Files

Every computer system has a different CONFIG.SYS file. The types of devices you have, the amount of memory you have, the way you like to use your computer—all these factors contribute to the way your CONFIG.SYS file looks. In this section, you look at some sample CONFIG.SYS files.

A typical CONFIG.SYS file for an 80386 computer with 2M or more of extended memory.

```
C:\>TYPE CONFIG.SYS
DEVICE=C:\DOS\HIMEM.SYS
DOS=HIGH,UMB
DEVICE=C:\DOS\EMM386.EXE RAM
FILES=40
BUFFERS=20
BREAK=ON
DEVICEHIGH=C:\DOS\ANSI.SYS

C:\>
```

In this example, note the following points:

- The DEVICE commands load the HIMEM.SYS and EMM386.EXE device drivers. The HIMEM.SYS driver manages extended memory. The EMM386.EXE driver, when used in a DEVICE= statement with the RAM switch, provides access to the upper memory area and simulates expanded memory.

■ The DOS=HIGH,UMB command runs PC DOS in the high memory area and specifies that programs should have access to the upper memory area. For more information about the upper memory area, see the section "Making More Memory Available," later in this chapter.

■ The FILES command reserves enough room to have 40 files open at one time.

■ The BUFFERS command reserves 20 buffers for transferring information to and from disk drives.

■ The BREAK command checks frequently for the Ctrl+C or Ctrl+Break key combination.

■ The DEVICEHIGH command loads a device driver into the upper memory area.

If you use a network and your system includes an 80286 processor and expanded memory, your CONFIG.SYS file may look like this.

```
C:\>TYPE CONFIG.SYS
DEVICE=C:\EMSDRV\EMSDRV.SYS
DEVICEHIGH=C:\DOS\HIMEM.SYS
DEVICE=C:\NET\NETWORK.SYS
DEVICE=C:\DOS\RAMDROVE.SYS /a
FILES=30
BUFFERS=20
BREAK=ON
LASTDRIVE=Z


C:\>
```

In this example, note the following points:

■ This CONFIG.SYS file loads device drivers for the expanded memory board, the HIMEM.SYS memory manager, and the network.

■ The RAMDRIVE.SYS driver creates a RAM drive in expanded memory.

8

■ The LASTDRIVE command reserves space for 26 logical drives so that letters from A through Z are available as names for drives.

Note: *You can use a single CONFIG.SYS file to set several different system configurations. This capability can be useful if several people share a single computer or if you want to be able to start your computer with a choice of configurations. For information on defining a CONFIG.SYS file for multiple configurations, see the section "Using Multiple System Configurations," later in this chapter.*

Viewing and Editing Your AUTOEXEC.BAT File

You can view the contents of your AUTOEXEC.BAT file by using the PC DOS TYPE command. To display the contents of your AUTOEXEC.BAT file on-screen, follow these steps:

1. At the PC DOS command prompt, type

   TYPE AUTOEXEC.BAT

2. Press **Enter**. PC DOS displays your AUTOEXEC.BAT file on-screen.

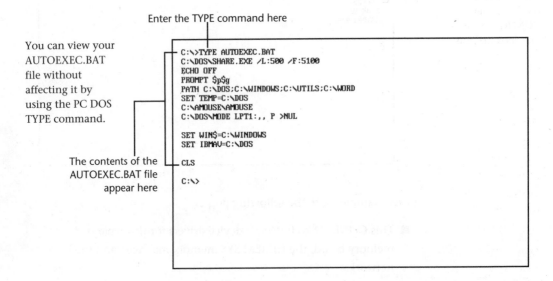

Enter the TYPE command here

You can view your AUTOEXEC.BAT file without affecting it by using the PC DOS TYPE command.

```
C:\>TYPE AUTOEXEC.BAT
C:\DOS\SHARE.EXE /L:500 /F:5100
ECHO OFF
PROMPT $p$g
PATH C:\DOS;C:\WINDOWS;C:\UTILS;C:\WORD
SET TEMP=C:\DOS
C:\AMOUSE\AMOUSE
C:\DOS\MODE LPT1:,, P >NUL

SET WINS=C:\WINDOWS
SET IBMAV=C:\DOS

CLS

C:\>
```

The contents of the AUTOEXEC.BAT file appear here

Your AUTOEXEC.BAT file can contain any command you can type at the PC DOS command prompt. By adding commands to AUTOEXEC.BAT, you can customize the way your system starts and runs.

You can edit the AUTOEXEC.BAT file using a text editor, such as the E Editor, that can save files as unformatted (ASCII) text. Do not edit the AUTOEXEC.BAT file using a word processing program that saves files in a document format. If you do, PC DOS will not be able to read the file, and your computer will not start. You can use a word processing program that saves files in ASCII format. For information on using the E Editor, see Chapter 7, "Working with the Text Editor."

Note: *Before changing your original AUTOEXEC.BAT file, make a copy, and save it with a different name, such as AUTOEXEC.BAK, as a precaution.*

To add a command to your AUTOEXEC.BAT file, follow these steps:

1. Open the file with the E Editor.

2. On a separate line, type the command the same way you would type it at the PC DOS command prompt. If necessary, include the complete path to the command file and all necessary command parameters.

3. Save the file.

4. Exit the E Editor.

5. Reboot your computer so that PC DOS executes the new commands.

Using and Customizing Your AUTOEXEC.BAT File

Memory-resident program
A software program, often a utility, that is stored in RAM as long as it is open for use. Sometimes called terminate-and-stay resident (TSR).

Each time you start your system, PC DOS carries out the commands in your AUTOEXEC.BAT file, which is located in the root directory of your hard disk (usually drive C). You can run AUTOEXEC.BAT the same way you run any batch file without restarting your computer. To run AUTOEXEC.BAT from the PC DOS command prompt, type **AUTOEXEC** and press **Enter**.

The commands in the AUTOEXEC.BAT file set the characteristics of your devices, customize information that PC DOS displays, and start *memory-resident programs* and other application programs.

8

Screen attributes

The way information is displayed on-screen, including colors, typeface and character enhancements, such as boldface and italics.

Every command in an AUTOEXEC.BAT file can also be used in other batch programs or issued directly from the PC DOS command prompt. Usually, AUTOEXEC.BAT files are used to run start-up commands, launch memory-resident programs, and change *screen attributes*.

For more specific information about these commands, type **HELP** followed by the command name at the PC DOS command prompt for a brief explanation and the command syntax.

Start-Up Commands

Table 8.1 describes some of the most common start-up commands used in AUTOEXEC.BAT files.

Table 8.1 Common AUTOEXEC.BAT Commands	
Command	**Purpose**
PROMPT	Sets the appearance of the PC DOS command prompt.
MODE	Sets the characteristics of the keyboard, display, and serial and parallel ports.
PATH	Specifies the directories in which PC DOS searches for executable files (files with a COM, EXE, or BAT file name extension).
ECHO OFF	Directs PC DOS not to display the commands in the AUTOEXEC.BAT file as they run. You can also prevent a command from being displayed by inserting an "at sign" (@) at the beginning of that line.
SET	Creates an environment variable that can be used by programs. The SET command can also be used in the CONFIG.SYS file.
CLS	Clears the screen of all information except the PC DOS command prompt.

Memory-Resident Programs

Another common use of the AUTOEXEC.BAT file is to start memory-resident, or TSR (terminate-and-stay-resident) programs—programs that load into memory and stay there while you use other programs.

PC DOS comes with several memory-resident programs that are commonly started from the AUTOEXEC.BAT file, including the following:

APPEND	FASTOPEN
CPSCHED	KEYB
DATAMON SENTRY (or TRACKER)	MOUSE
DOSKEY	SMARTDRV

Screen Attributes

ANSI set graphics mode access sequence
A command statement that defines standard screen display settings.

You can change your *screen attributes* by using the PROMPT command and an *ANSI set graphics mode access sequence* in your AUTOEXEC.BAT file.

Note: *The ANSI.SYS driver must be loaded in your CONFIG.SYS file if you plan to use an ANSI set graphics mode access sequence in your AUTOEXEC.BAT file.*

There are three kinds of screen attributes:

■ *Text format.* Specifies whether text is bold, underscored, blinking, or hidden.

■ *Text color.* Specifies the text color.

■ *Background color.* Specifies the screen color.

To change screen attributes, follow these steps:

1. Open the AUTOEXEC.BAT file using the E Editor.

Note: *You can have two prompt commands in the AUTOEXEC.BAT file—one to control the information displayed in the PC DOS command prompt and one to control the screen attributes.*

8

2. On a separate line, type the PROMPT command as follows:

PROMPT $E[$x;xx;xx$M

In this command syntax,

$E indicates the ANSI access code

x indicates the number that controls the text format

xx indicates the number that controls the text color

xxM indicates the numbers that control the screen color, followed by the number that indicates the ANSI set graphics mode

The order in which you type the parameters is not important. However, the parameters must be separated by semicolons.

To identify the text format (x), use one of the following options:

1   Changes the text to BOLD, or high intensity.

4   Changes the text to underscored. This option works on monochrome displays only.

5   Changes the text so that it blinks.

7   Changes the screen display to reverse video. Reverse video reverses the foreground and background colors or shades used on the screen. For example, if your screen normally displays dark letters on a light background, reverse video displays light letters against a dark background.

8   Hides the text unless you subsequently change the background color.

To identify the text color (*xx*), use one of the following options:

30	Black
31	Red
32	Green
33	Yellow
34	Blue
35	Magenta
36	Cyan
37	White

To identify the background color (*xx*M), use one of the following:

40	Black
41	Red
42	Green
43	Yellow
44	Blue
45	Magenta
46	Cyan
47	White

If you have problems...   If nothing happens to your screen display after you enter the PROMPT statement and reboot your system, you probably entered a parameter that your computer system does not support. The system ignores the statement, and no change takes place.

8

This
AUTOEXEC.BAT
file includes
commands to
show yellow text
on a red back-
ground in bold or
high intensity.

The PROMPT command that
controls the contents of the
PC DOS command prompt

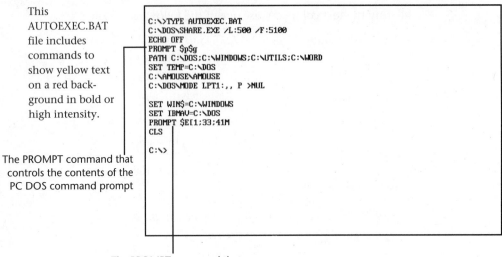

```
C:\>TYPE AUTOEXEC.BAT
C:\DOS\SHARE.EXE /L:500 /F:5100
ECHO OFF
PROMPT $p$g
PATH C:\DOS;C:\WINDOWS;C:\UTILS;C:\WORD
SET TEMP=C:\DOS
C:\AMOUSE\AMOUSE
C:\DOS\MODE LPT1:,, P >NUL

SET WIN$=C:\WINDOWS
SET IBMAV=C:\DOS
PROMPT $E[1;33;41M
CLS

C:\>
```

The PROMPT command that
controls screen attributes

Sample AUTOEXEC.BAT Files

Every computer system has a different AUTOEXEC.BAT file. The
memory-resident programs you have, the start-up commands you want
to use, and the way you like to use your computer—all these factors contribute to the way your AUTOEXEC.BAT file looks. This section presents
two sample AUTOEXEC.BAT files.

This
AUTOEXEC.BAT
file contains some
of the most
commonly used
commands.

```
C:\>TYPE AUTOEXEC.BAT
PATH=C:\;C:\DOS;C:\WINDOWS;C:\UTILITY;C:\BATCH
PROMPT $p$g
SET TEMP=C:\DOS
DOSKEY
C:\DOS\SMARTDRV.EXE

C:\>
```

In the preceding example, note the following points:

■ The PATH command directs PC DOS to search for program files in the current directory and then in the following directories: the root directory of drive C, C:\DOS, C:\WINDOWS, C:\UTILITY, and C:\BATCH. A semicolon (;) sets off each directory.

■ The PROMPT command sets the command prompt so that it shows the current drive and directory followed by a greater-than sign (>).

■ The SET command creates an environment variable named TEMP and sets it equal to the directory C:\DOS.

Note: *When you set a temporary environment, the name you specify must be the name of an existing directory.*

■ The DOSKEY command loads the DOSKey program into memory. DOSKEY.COM can be located in any directory listed in the PATH command.

■ The SMARTDRV command loads the SMARTDrive program into memory.

A typical AUTOEXEC.BAT file for a system with one diskette drive, one hard disk drive, a laser printer connected to port COM1, and Windows.

```
C:\>TYPE AUTOEXEC.BAT
@ECHO OFF
PATH=C:\;C:\DOS;C:\WINDOWS;C:\UTILITY;C:\WORD;C:\EXCEL
PROMPT $p$g
MODE LPT1=COM1
SET TEMP=C:\DOS
DOSKEY
WIN

C:\>
```

8

In the preceding example, note the following points:

- The ECHO OFF command prevents the AUTOEXEC.BAT commands from being displayed as they are carried out. The @ sign at the beginning of the line prevents the ECHO OFF command itself from being displayed.

- The MODE command redirects printer output from LPT1 (its default port) to the serial port COM1.

- The DOSKEY command loads the DOSKey program, which provides keyboard shortcuts at the PC DOS command prompt.

- The WIN command starts Windows.

Using Multiple System Configurations

You can use a single CONFIG.SYS file to set several different system configurations. This capability can be useful if several people share a single computer or if you want to be able to start your computer with a choice of configurations.

Defining multiple configuration commands can consist of four procedures:

- Define configuration blocks in your CONFIG.SYS file.

- Define a start-up menu in your CONFIG.SYS file.

- Use INCLUDE statements in your CONFIG.SYS file.

- Modify the AUTOEXEC.BAT file.

Configuration block
A grouped set of CONFIG.SYS commands used to specify multiple start-up configurations.

Defining Configuration Blocks

A *configuration block* is a grouped set of CONFIG.SYS commands. A configuration block can contain any command you normally put in your CONFIG.SYS file.

Block header
The name of the configuration block, enclosed in brackets and typed on the first line of the configuration block.

To specify a configuration block, you type a *block header*—the block name enclosed by brackets—and then you type the commands you want included in the group, each command on its own line.

The block name must be a single word but can be as long as you want. Some typical block names are the following:

- *[MENU]*. Used to define a start-up menu.

- *[COMMON]*. Used to define a block of commands common to all configurations.

INCLUDE is used to define a block that includes a previously defined block.

When PC DOS comes to a block in a CONFIG.SYS file, PC DOS carries out all the commands between the block header and the next block header, or the end of the file.

This part of a CONFIG.SYS file defines three configurations and includes several commands that are common to both.

```
[CPSW]
COUNTRY=001,,C:\DOS\COUNTRY.SYS
DEVICEHIGH=C:\DOS\DISPLAY.SYS CON=(EGA,,1)
[DLS]
DEVICEHIGH=C:\NET\PROTMAN.DOS /i:C:\NET
DEVICEHIGH=C:\NET\IBMTOK.DOS
[INTLNK]
DEVICEHIGH=C:DOS\INTERLNK.EXE
[COMMON]
DEVICEHIGH=C:DOS\ANSI.SYS
SHELL=C:\DOS\COMMAND.COM /P/E:512
FILES=30
BUFFERS=30
LASTDRIVE=Z
BREAK=ON
DEVICE=C:\DOS\HIMEM.SYS
DOS=HIGH,UMB
DEVICE=C:\DOS\EMM386.EXE NOEMS
DEVICE=C:\DATA\SETVER.EXE
```

This CONFIG.SYS file configures the computer for code page switching and keyboard support [CPSW], LAN networking [DLS], and laptop computer connectivity [INTLNK]. For all three configurations, PC DOS runs the commands in the [COMMON] configuration block.

8

Defining a Start-Up Menu

At the beginning of the CONFIG.SYS file with multiple configurations, you should define a start-up menu. To do this, create a configuration block with the block heading [MENU]. A menu block can contain any of the following commands:

- *MENUITEM*. Used to define each item on the menu.

- *MENUDEFAULT*. Used to specify the default configuration.

- *MENUCOLOR*. Used to set the text color.

- *SUBMENU*. Used to define submenu items, if necessary.

- *NUMLOCK*. Can be set to On or Off.

When your computer starts, the start-up menu appears and lists the available configurations. You are prompted to choose the configuration you want.

A sample start-up menu is defined for the configurations shown in the preceding section.

```
[MENU]
MENUITEM=DLS, LOAD DOS LAN SERVICES CLIENT
MENUITEM=INTLNK, LOAD INTERLNK CLIENT
MENUITEM=CPSW, LOAD CODE PAGE SWITCHING
MENUCOLOR=7,1
MENUDEFAULT=DLS,20
NUMLOCK=OFF
```

In this example, note the following:

- The MENUITEM command specifies each of three possible configurations. The first MENUITEM command value specifies the configuration block header. The second value, which is optional, specifies the text to display on the menu. If you do not specify any menu text, PC DOS uses the name of the configuration block as the menu text.

- The MENUCOLOR command sets the text color to 7 (white) and the background color to 1 (royal blue).

- The MENUDEFAULT command is optional. It specifies which menu item is to be the default configuration. When PC DOS displays the start-up menu, the default menu item is highlighted, and its number appears after the `Enter a choice` prompt. If no item is specified, the default is set to the first item.

Timeout value

The amount of time PC DOS will wait for the user to select a menu item. If nothing is selected in this time, PC DOS selects the default item.

Note: *With the MENUDEFAULT command, you can also specify a timeout value. You can specify a timeout value from 0 through 90 seconds. If the user does not select an item within the specified time, PC DOS selects the default item. In this example, the timeout value is 20 seconds.*

Using INCLUDE Statements

The CONFIG.SYS file can also contain the INCLUDE command, which enables you to include the contents of one configuration block in another block.

The INCLUDE command instructs PC DOS to carry out the commands in another configuration block as well as the commands in the current block. INCLUDE can be used only within a configuration block.

Suppose that you want to add another configuration which combines all three of the previously discussed configuration blocks. You can use the INCLUDE command to do this by adding a fourth configuration similar to the following

A fourth user-specified configuration name, called [LOADALL], is defined. It uses the INCLUDE menu command to combine all three of the other configurations.

```
[LOADALL]
INCLUDE=CPSW
INCLUDE=DLS
INCLUDE=INTLNK

[COMMON]
SET PATH=C:\NET\C:\DOS.
```

8

Note: *Placing a [COMMON] block at the end of your CONFIG.SYS file is a good practice, even if the block does not contain any commands. Some application programs append commands to your CONFIG.SYS file. If your CONFIG.SYS file has a [COMMON] block at the end, an application program can append commands to the CONFIG.SYS, and PC DOS will carry out those commands for all your configurations. If you do not want them carried out for all your configurations, you should manually enter the commands into the appropriate configuration blocks.*

Modifying the AUTOEXEC.BAT File

When you use multiple configurations, you may want to set PC DOS to run different AUTOEXEC.BAT commands for each configuration. You can create branching code in the AUTOEXEC.BAT file by using batch commands, such as the IF and GOTO commands. With batch commands, you can have PC DOS carry out different AUTOEXEC.BAT commands depending on the start-up configuration.

When the user selects a configuration from the start-up menu, PC DOS sets the CONFIG environment variable to the name of the selected configuration block. In the AUTOEXEC.BAT file, you can use the IF command to test the value of the CONFIG variable and then have PC DOS carry out different commands for different values.

When you test the value of the CONFIG variable, you enclose it in both percent marks (%) and double quotation marks (”), as shown in the following example. For information about the IF command, type **HELP IF** at the PC DOS command prompt.

The AUTOEXEC.BAT file tests the CONFIG variable and runs different commands depending on the result of the test.

```
@ECHO OFF
PATH C:\DOS;C:\NET;
PROMPT $p$g
SET TEMP=C:\DOS

IF "%CONFIG%" == "DLS" C:\NET\NET START

IF NOT "%CONFIG%" == "CPSW" GOTO NOTCPSW
MODE CON CODEPAGE PREPARE=((850)) C:\DOS\ISO.CPI)
MODE CON CODEPAGE SELECT=850
LOADHIGH KEYB US

:NOTCPSW
CHOICE /C:YN /TN,3 Do you want to load MOUSE support?
IF ERRORLEVEL 2 GOTO SKIPMOUSE
LOADHIGH C:\DOS\MOUSE.COM

:SKIPMOUSE
LOADHIGH DOSKEY
SETIBMAV=C:\DOS
C:\DOS\
CALL C:\DOS\IBMAVDR.BAT C:\DOS\


C:\>
```

When PC DOS runs this AUTOEXEC.BAT file, it sets the path, command prompt style, and the TEMP environment variable.

PC DOS then tests the value of the CONFIG variable. The CONFIG.SYS value was set when you entered your choice of configuration from the start-up menu.

In the example, if the name of the current configuration is not CPSW, PC DOS inquires whether you want mouse support. If you do not want to load the mouse or you do not make a choice within three seconds, mouse support will not be loaded.

Whether or not you choose to have mouse support, this configuration then runs the DOSKey program and starts IBM AntiVirus/DOS.

Analyzing Your Computer's Memory

Programs that run with PC DOS normally use your system's conventional memory. Many programs can also use extended or expanded memory if it is available. If your system has an 80386-based or higher processor, you can also run programs in the upper memory area. You have two ways to find out about your computer's memory—the MEM and QCONFIG commands.

The MEM Command

You can use the MEM command to display a status report that details the type of memory your system has, how much memory is in use, and which programs are currently loaded into each type of memory.

To display a MEM status report, type **MEM** at the PC DOS command prompt, and press **Enter**.

8

The MEM
command displays
a status report of
memory configura-
tion and usage.

```
C:\>MEM

Memory Type      Total  =  Used  +  Free
--------------------------------------------
Conventional      640K      99K     541K
Upper             160K      49K     111K
Reserved          384K     384K       0K
Extended (XMS)  2,912K     212K   2,700K
--------------------------------------------
Total memory    4,096K     744K   3,352K

Total under 1Mb   800K     148K     652K

Largest executable program size     541K (553,632 bytes)
Largest free upper memory block     109K (111,136 bytes)
PC DOS is resident in the high memory area.

C:\>
```

To display a status report that includes a list of programs currently loaded
in memory, follow these steps:

1. At the PC DOS command prompt, type **MEM /C/P**.

    The /C switch tells PC DOS to list programs currently loaded in
    memory. The /P switch tells PC DOS to pause at the bottom of each
    screen of information.

2. Press **Enter**.

A list of programs
loaded in memory
is included in the
status report.

```
Modules using memory below 1Mb:

Name       Total      =  Conventional  +  Upper Memory
-------------------------------------------------------------
IBMDOS    13,437  (13K)   13,437  (13K)       0    (0K)
HIMEM      1,120   (1K)    1,120   (1K)       0    (0K)
EMM386     3,072   (3K)    3,072   (3K)       0    (0K)
RAMBOOST  10,832  (11K)      320   (0K)  10,512   (10K)
COMMAND    2,928   (3K)    2,928   (3K)       0    (0K)
SAVE      80,736  (79K)   80,736  (79K)       0    (0K)
SHARE     17,008  (17K)        0   (0K)  17,008   (17K)
AMOUSE    13,024  (13K)        0   (0K)  13,024   (13K)
MODE         480   (0K)        0   (0K)     480    (0K)
FREE     667,264 (652K)  553,728 (541K) 113,536  (111K)

Memory summary:

Type of Memory   Total      =  Used      +  Free
-------------------------------------------------------------
Conventional      655,360      101,632      553,728
Upper             163,824       50,288      113,536
Reserved          393,216      393,216            0
Extended (XMS)  2,981,904      217,104    2,764,800
Press any key to continue...
```

The QCONFIG Command

Alternatively, you can use the QCONFIG command to find out what kind of memory your system has and how much is available for your application programs. QCONFIG is a utility used to query information about your computer system. It displays a complete status report, including information about memory.

To use the QCONFIG command, follow these steps:

1. At the PC DOS command prompt, type

QCONFIG /P

The /P switch instructs PC DOS to pause at the bottom of each screen of information.

2. Press **Enter**. QCONFIG examines your system and displays an analysis on-screen.

At the bottom of the QCONFIG analysis, you can find information about memory usage.

Device information appears here

Memory information appears here

```
Keyboard Type    : Enhanced
Pointer Type     : Serial Mouse  Buttons: 2  Int Level: 4
Pointer Version  : 6.16
Equipment        : 1 Parallel Port(s)
                 : 2 Serial Port(s)
                 : 2 Diskette Drive(s)
                 : 1 Fixed Disk(s)
                 : Pointing Device
                 : Math CoProcessor
Serial Port 1    : COM1: 03F8
Serial Port 2    : COM2: 02E8
Parallel Port 1  : LPT1: 0378
Primary Video    : VGA
Diskette Drive 1: 5.25"  - 1.2M - 80 Track - Type 2
Diskette Drive 2: 3.50"  - 1.44M - 80 Track - Type 4
Fixed Disk 1     :   81 MB  =   83215 KB  =   85212160 bytes  Type 47
Logical Drive C : Size   83026K =   81.0M Avail    3272K =    3.1M
Total Memory     :  3712 KB = 3.6 MB
Conventional     :   640 KB  Free:    541 KB
Extended Memory  :  3072 KB  Free:      0 KB
XMS Memory       :  2700 KB  Free:  2700 KB
XMS Version      : 3.0
Adapter ROM 1    : Addr C0000-C7FFF Phoenix

C:\>
```

You can save the information from the QCONFIG analysis so that you have a description of your current system configuration. You can print the file, using the E Editor. For information on using the E Editor, see Chapter 7, "Working with the Text Editor."

8

To save the QCONFIG analysis to a file, take one of the following steps:

■ At the PC DOS command prompt, type **QCONFIG /O** to direct the information to a file named QCONFIG.OUT

■ At the PC DOS command prompt, type **QCONFIG /O***filename.ext* to direct the information displayed to a text file of your choice.

If you have problems...

If you try to direct the output to a file of your choice, but PC DOS displays the following message, you left a space between the /O switch and the file name.

```
Argument ignored - 'filename.ext'
Output redirected to file 'QCONFIG.OUT'
```

Note: *For more information about the QCONFIG command, type **HELP QCONFIQ** at the PC DOS command prompt.*

Making More Memory Available

To run a program, your system must contain as much physical memory as that program requires. Some programs require more memory than others. If you do not have enough memory to run a program, you can take one of two actions:

■ You can increase the amount of physical memory on your system by plugging a memory board into a slot inside your computer.

■ You can adjust your computer's configuration to make more of your existing memory available to programs.

Some programs do not run even if your system does contain sufficient physical memory. The cause is often that memory-resident programs are taking up some memory and not enough memory is left over. Changing your memory configuration can help make memory available by changing the way the computer allocates memory usage.

PC DOS comes with a memory optimizer utility program called RAMBoost. RAMBoost automatically adjusts your computer's configuration to make the best possible use of all available memory.

Using RAMBoost

RAMBoost is a memory optimizer utility program that automatically adjusts your memory configuration to optimize memory usage.

When you run the RAMBoost Setup program, it analyzes your current configuration and then makes the necessary adjustments to increase your computer's available conventional memory.

After RAMBoost is installed, RAMBoost analyzes your computer's existing configuration and automatically reconfigures programs to load into upper memory every time you start your computer.

RAMBoost manages the Upper Memory Block (UMB) of your computer from 640K to 1,024K. RAMBoost runs invisibly on your computer, optimizing available memory automatically each time your computer's system configuration changes.

If you add or remove programs from your CONFIG.SYS file or AUTOEXEC.BAT file, RAMBoost automatically detects the change, reboots, and rearranges the remaining drivers in upper memory.

Memory manager
A utility program that makes the open areas in your upper memory blocks available for loading memory-resident programs and device drivers.

RAMBoost works with a *memory manager* to load device drivers and utility programs into upper memory in order to make more conventional memory available for running application programs.

If you are familiar with memory-management techniques, you can customize RAMBoost's performance by manually editing the settings in the RAMBOOST.INI file.

For example, RAMBoost detects software that can cause incompatibilities when loaded into upper or high memory. In some cases, you might gain more conventional memory by manually shifting the position of the memory manager in the CONFIG.SYS file; however, this change generally is not necessary.

8

Understanding RAMBoost System Requirements

To use RAMBoost Setup, your system must meet the following requirements:

- A minimum of 512K extended memory

- An 80386-based, 80486-based, or higher processor

- For Upper Memory Block support, at least 640K and an EEMS/EMS 4.0 memory manager

RAMBoost supports the following EEMS/EMS 4.0 memory managers:

HIMEM.SYS and EMM386.EXE provided with PC DOS

Quarterdeck Expanded Memory Manager-386

Qualitas 386MAX and BlueMAX

Helix Netroom

Configuring RAMBoost

You configure RAMBoost by running the RAMBoost Setup program.

Before you configure RAMBoost, make the following preparations:

- Make sure that all adapter cards installed on your computer are loaded or activated. If you do not have your adapter activated, RAMBoost Setup will incorrectly use the adapter memory space.

- When you are using QEMM386, 386MAX, or Netroom, you must install it according to its installation instructions and make sure that it provides upper memory blocks.

- Make backup copies of your CONFIG.SYS and AUTOEXEC.BAT files as a precaution.

- Remove all INSTALLHIGH statements from your CONFIG.SYS file.

- Use the MEM command to save information about your memory to an output file so that you can compare it later to see the results you get after you have loaded RAMBoost.

If you have problems...

To save the output of the MEM command, type **MEM /C > *filename.ext*** at the PC DOS command prompt. The MEM command is preferable to QCONFIG in this case because MEM gives more details about your programs' upper memory.

To configure RAMBoost, follow these steps:

1. At the PC DOS command prompt, type **RAMSETUP**.

2. Press **Enter**. The RAMBoost dialog box appears.

RAMBoost analyzes your system configuration and recommends a course of action. Here, it recommends removing the EMM386 statement from the CONFIG.SYS file.

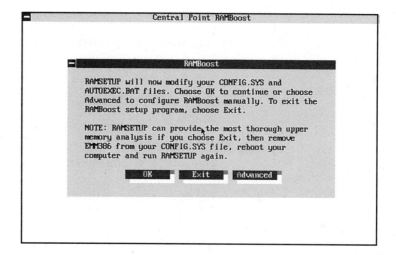

3. Follow the instructions that RAMBoost displays on-screen.

If RAMBoost Setup detects a DEVICE=EMM386.EXE statement in your CONFIG.SYS file, you should select Exit; remove or use the REM command to comment the DEVICE=EMM386.EXE statement; reboot your system; and then run RAMBoost Setup again. Removing this statement provides the most thorough upper memory analysis.

After RAMBOOST no longer detects DEVICE=EMM386, any of the following scenarios is possible, depending on what programs exist in your CONFIG.SYS file when RAMBoost Setup is run:

8

- If RAMBoost Setup detects that you have a PC DOS memory manager installed, RAMBoost Setup installs RAMBoost in your CONFIG.SYS file. Then you can go to step 4.

- If RAMBoost Setup detects that you have installed a memory manager other than the one in PC DOS, RAMBoost Setup installs RAMBoost in your CONFIG.SYS file and may modify your AUTOEXEC.BAT file by removing any LOADHIGH or DEVICEHIGH statements. RAMBoost does not recognize the INSTALLHIGH statement, so you should make sure that any INSTALLHIGH statements are removed before running RAMBoost Setup. Then you can go to step 4.

- If RAMBoost Setup detects that you have no memory manager installed but finds the PC DOS memory manager on your computer, RAMBoost Setup installs RAMBoost and the memory manager in your CONFIG.SYS file. Then you can go to step 4.

- If RAMBoost Setup cannot find a memory manager on your computer, it informs you that you must install one.

4. After RAMBoost Setup installs RAMBoost in your CONFIG.SYS file, the following screen appears.

You have the option of reconfiguring the PC DOS memory manager to its base settings or modifying your computer's upper memory blocks manually.

Click to have RAMBoost reconfigure the PC DOS memory manager

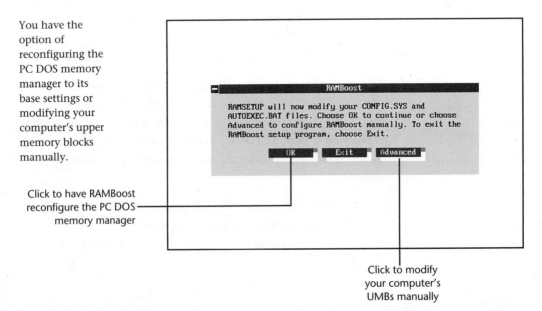

Click to modify your computer's UMBs manually

5. Choose OK to have RAMBoost automatically reconfigure the PC
   DOS memory manager. RAMBoost prompts you to reboot your
   computer. During this reboot, RAMBoost analyzes your current
   configuration to determine the best usage of upper memory.

As you watch your computer screen, you see RAMBoost boot your computer and run the CONFIG.SYS and AUTOEXEC.BAT files. You do not
have to take any action. You will see a prompt for loading RAMBoost
appear on-screen, but you should not respond to it.

When the reboot is complete, RAMBoost reboots the computer again.
Finally, RAMBoost displays the PC DOS command prompt. RAMBoost
has optimized your memory configuration. You should notice an increase in the amount of available memory.

Understanding the RAMBoost Learn Mode

When analyzing a new system configuration, RAMBoost operates in learn
mode. If you watch your computer screen during RAMBoost configuration or during start-up, you will see a message indicating that RAMBoost
is running in learn mode.

In learn mode, the RAMBoost program is working to determine the opti-
mal location for every object loaded since (and including) the loading of
RAMBoost. This process can be long. A feature of the RAMBoost program
is a progress bar that shows the current status of the Learn function.

The progress bar indicates the actual percentage of the possible combinations that have been examined. The time display provides an estimate of
how much longer the processing may take. This estimate is based on how
long it has taken to process the current fraction of the job.

You can bypass the learn mode at any time. This capability can be useful
if you change your AUTOEXEC.BAT and CONFIG.SYS files frequently.

To bypass the learn mode, follow these steps:

1. At the PC DOS command prompt, type **RAMBOOST SYNC**.

2. PC DOS asks for confirmation that you want to bypass the learn
   mode. Choose **Y**.

8

Analyzing Your Computer's Memory after Running RAMBoost

After RAMBoost is loaded, you can check to see whether you really do have more conventional memory available.

One way to check that RAMBoost has been successful is to use the TYPE command to display your CONFIG.SYS file. (For more information, see the section "Viewing and Editing Your CONFIG.SYS File," earlier in this chapter.)

If your CONFIG.SYS file has commands with INCLUDE and EXCLUDE statements and if a RAMBOOST statement appears, you can assume that RAMBoost has been loaded successfully.

```
C:\>TYPE CONFIG.SYS
device=C:\DOS\HIMEM.SYS
device=c:\dos\emm386.exe noems ram x=a000-b0ff i=b100-b7ff x=b800-c7ff i=c800-ef
device=c:\dos\ramboost.exe load
REM DEVICE=C:\DOS\EMM386.EXE NOEMS
BUFFERS= 20,0
FILES=50
LASTDRIVE=E
FCBS=16,8
DEVICE=C:\DOS\SETVER.EXE
dos=high
SHELL=C:\DOS\COMMAND.COM C:\DOS\ /p
STACKS=9,256
REM DEVICEHIGH /L:1,34592 =C:\MOUSE.SYS

C:\>
```

The RAMBOOST statement

This line shows INCLUDE and EXCLUDE statements

Another way to check your memory usage is to use the MEM command to save information about your memory to an output file and compare it to the analysis of memory you made before you loaded RAMBoost. For information on saving the output of the MEM command, see the section "Analyzing Your Computer's Memory," earlier in this chapter.

Check free
conventional
memory here

In the MEM status
report, you can see
whether RAMBoost
has made a
difference in
the amount of
available conven-
tional memory.

```
C:\>MEM

Memory Type      Total  =  Used  +  Free

Conventional      640K      99K      541K
Upper             252K     113K      139K
Reserved          384K     384K        0K
Extended (XMS)  2,820K     180K    2,640K

Total memory    4,096K     776K    3,320K

Total under 1Mb   892K     212K      680K

Largest executable program size      541K (553,632 bytes)
Largest free upper memory block      134K (136,768 bytes)
PC DOS is resident in the high memory area.

C:\>
```

Using RAMBoost with Other Programs

The following information tells you how to use RAMBoost with specific programs and memory managers.

Helix Netroom386

If you use Helix Netroom386, make sure that the following statement is in your CONFIG.SYS file before you start RAMBoost:

```
device=c:\netroom\rm386.sys ems=c800-efff frame=none
```

Note: *This statement assumes that you are not using EMS.*

Qualitas 386MAX and BlueMAX

If you use Qualitas 386MAX and BlueMAX, the following statement should be in your CONFIG.SYS file before you start RAMBoost:

```
device=c:\max\386max.sys include=b000-b800 ems=512
```

If you do not need EMS, change the EMS parameter to read ems=0. Making this change increases the upper memory available to RAMBoost by 64K.

8

If RAMBoost Setup detects 386MAX (Version 7 or later) or detects BlueMax (Version 6.02 or later), RAMBoost Setup adds the NO58 parameter to the MAX profile. If you install one of these versions after RAMBoost is loaded, you will need to edit the MAX profile manually or run RAMBoost Setup again.

Any version of 386MAX or BlueMAX before the version listed should not include the NO58 parameter in the MAX profile.

RAMBoost Setup deletes from the CONFIG.SYS file two incompatible BlueMAX or 386MAX (Version 7) devices, both named EXTRADOS.MAX.

QEMM-386

If QEMM-386 is already installed, you should see the following statement in your CONFIG.SYS file:

```
device=c:qemm\qemm386.sys ram x=f000-ffff st:m
```

If you do not need EMS, add the NOEMS parameter to this statement in your CONFIG.SYS file. Making this change increases the upper memory available to RAMBoost by 64K.

RAMBoost Setup deletes the following incompatible QEMM (Version 7) devices from the CONFIG.SYS file:

DOS-UP.SYS

DOSDATA.SYS

DESQview and Enhanced Windows

RAMBoost does not automatically reset from the DESQview DOS box or the enhanced Windows environment. You must reset it manually.

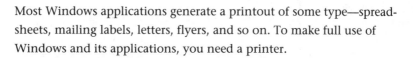

Chapter 9

Controlling the Printer

Most Windows applications generate a printout of some type—spreadsheets, mailing labels, letters, flyers, and so on. To make full use of Windows and its applications, you need a printer.

When you install Windows, you choose the printer you want to use with your applications. You can change that printer or select a different printer at any time.

Font
A specific size and style of character that can be displayed on-screen or output to your printer.

In addition to understanding how to use different printers in Windows, you need to understand the different *fonts* that are available. In Chapter 5, "Using File Manager," you learned to change the font used to display the File Manager on-screen. You also can change the fonts used to print.

In this chapter, you learn to use the Windows Print Manager to set up and control the printing of your files. You also learn about using different fonts.

Understanding the Print Manager

The Print Manager comes with Windows and controls printing functions for all Windows applications. Print Manager runs in the background, which means that you can use other applications while files are printing.

You don't actually use the Print Manager to initiate printing. You must issue print commands specific to the Windows application you are using to print the file. To print a file in most Windows applications, choose **F**ile, **P**rint.

The Print Manager starts automatically whenever you print a file from a Windows application. When the Print Manager is active, the Print Manager icon appears on the desktop beneath the application window.

In this figure, the Print Manager icon appears at the lower left corner of the desktop because the Print Manager is active. Sometimes the icon is hidden behind another window.

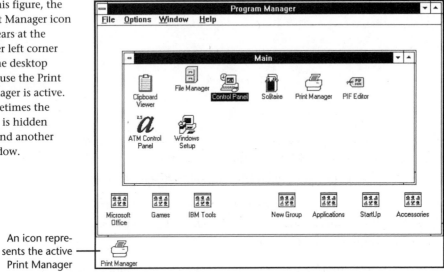

An icon represents the active Print Manager

To open the Print Manager window, take one of the following actions:

- Double-click the Print Manager icon on the desktop.

- Double-click the Print Manager icon in the Main group window.

- Press **Ctrl+Esc** to display the Task List, and then switch to the Print Manager.

If you have problems...

If the Print Manager doesn't start, double-click the Printer icon in the Control Panel window. Make sure that an *X* is in the Use Print Manager check box.

Click here to pause printing Click here to resume printing

In the Print Manager window, you can control the way your files are printed, and you can change printer setup options.

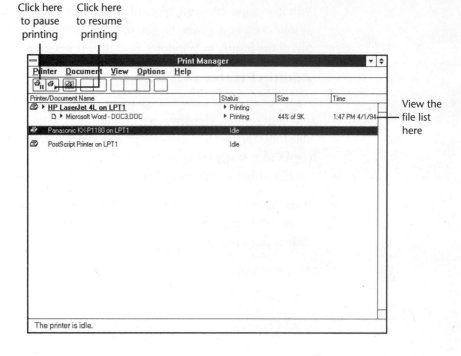

View the file list here

The Print Manager window lists the files waiting to be printed. You can pause the printing, cancel a print job, change the order of files in the print queue, and shift resource priorities between the computer and the printers.

Installing a Printer

Before you can print from Windows, you must install a printer. Usually you install your printer when you set up Windows. However, you can change printers or install new printers at any time.

Printer Driver
A file that gives Windows the printer information it needs to print properly.

Printer port
The external port on your computer to which your printer is attached.

Installing a printer in Windows means more than just connecting a printer to your computer. To install a printer in Windows, you must install a *printer driver*, select the *printer port*, and select any special print options you want to use. The following sections provide more details on these tasks. You can have more than one printer installed in Windows at any time, and the printers can be set up with different options. When you want to print a file, you can choose the printer you want to use for that particular print job.

9

Windows supports many types of printers—dot-matrix, inkjet, and laser, as well as other high-resolution, photo-typesetting printers. Before you install the printer in Windows, read the printer documentation.

Adding Printer Drivers

A printer driver acts like a language interpreter between the computer and your printer. The driver tells Windows such information as the available fonts, printer features, and printer control sequences. Windows comes with many common printer drivers you can use, or you can use a vendor-supplied diskette to load the printer driver into Windows.

Note: *To install a printer driver, you must have a diskette containing the printer driver for Windows. Use your original Windows 3.1 diskettes or the diskette that came from the printer manufacturer.*

To install a printer driver file, follow these steps:

1. Open the Print Manager window.

2. Choose **O**ptions, **P**rinter Setup. The Printers dialog box appears.

In the Printers dialog box, you can add new printers, remove currently installed printers, and change printer setup information.

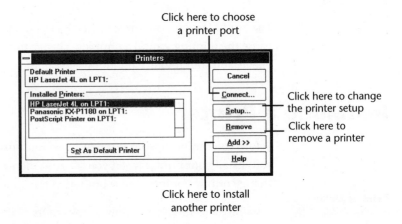

Click here to choose a printer port

Click here to change the printer setup

Click here to remove a printer

Click here to install another printer

3. In the Printers dialog box, choose **A**dd. The Print Manager displays a list of printers in the lower left corner of the expanded Printers dialog box.

Windows comes
with a list of
printers from
which you can
choose a printer
to install.

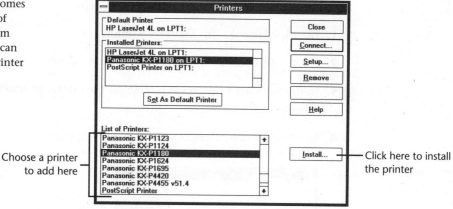

Choose a printer
to add here

Click here to install
the printer

4. From the **L**ist of Printers, choose the printer you want.

If you have **problems...**	If your printer doesn't appear on the list, choose Install Unlisted or Updated Printer, which appears at the top of the list.

5. Click **I**nstall. Windows adds the printer to the list of installed printers and may prompt you to insert a diskette. Continue to follow the
instructions displayed on-screen.

6. Click Close to close the Printers dialog box and return to the Print
Manager window.

Selecting a Printer Port

Printers connect to your computer by means of a cable attached to a
printer port. In order for Windows to print, you need to indicate to
which port your printer is attached. That port can be a parallel (LPT)
or a serial (COM) port. You select the port in the Printers dialog box.

If you have **problems...**	If you don't know to which port your printer cable is attached, look in your documentation or ask someone who does know, such as a support technician, or whoever helped you set up your computer.

9

To select a port for your printer, follow these steps:

1. Double-click the Print Manager window.

2. Choose **O**ptions, **P**rinter Setup. The Printers dialog box appears.

3. In the Installed **P**rinters list box, select the printer to which you want to assign a port.

4. Choose **C**onnect. The Connect dialog box appears.

In the Connect dialog box, select the port to which your printer is connected.

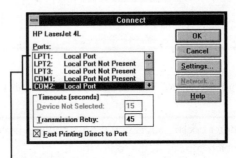

Select a port here

5. Select the correct printer port from the list of ports. Usually, the correct port is identified with the words *Local Port*.

6. Choose OK to return to the Printers dialog box.

Setting Printer Options

You can control the appearance of a document by changing printer setup and printing options.

To view or change your printer settings, follow these steps:

1. Double-click the Print Manager window.

2. Choose **O**ptions, **P**rinter Setup. The Printers dialog box appears.

3. In the Printers dialog box, choose **S**etup. The Setup dialog box appears.

Choose paper options here

In the Setup dialog box, you can choose such options as the paper size and orientation.

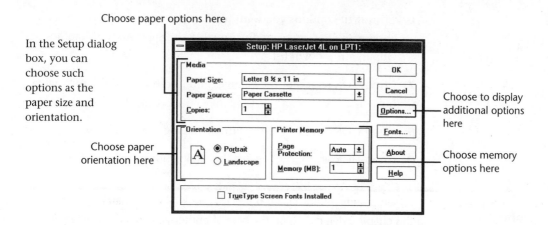

Choose paper orientation here

Choose to display additional options here

Choose memory options here

4. Choose the settings you want to change. For example, you can change the paper size by choosing a different size from the Paper Size drop-down list, and you can enter the number of copies you want to print in the Copies text box. To print the document vertically on the page, choose Portrait in the Orientation area; to print the document horizontally on the page, choose Landscape.

5. Choose **O**ptions to display the Options dialog box.

You can set additional printing options in the Options dialog box.

Choose graphics printing options here

Choose print quality options here

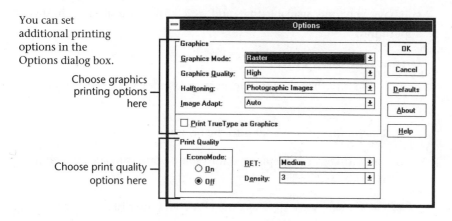

9

6. Choose the options you want to change. For example, you can choose an alternative graphics quality setting from the Graphics Quality drop-down list.

7. Choose OK to accept the changes and to return to the Setup dialog box.

8. Choose OK to return to the Printers dialog box.

9. Choose Close to close the Printers dialog box.

If you have problems... Your Setup and Options dialog boxes may look different than the ones used in this chapter, depending on the type of printer you are using. Different printers have different options. For information specific to your printer's printing options, consult your printer documentation.

Using Fonts

When you create a document in a Windows application, the appearance of the printed document depends on three factors: the type of printer you have, the fonts available to it, and which fonts you specified in the application.

Understanding Fonts

You can use three basic kinds of fonts with Windows and most Windows applications:

- *Resident* fonts come built into the printer.

- *Font cartridges* can be plugged into some printers to add to their list of resident fonts.

- *Soft fonts* are software files stored on your hard disk.

Scalable
A font that can be made very small or very large without introducing distortions.

In addition to using the resident and other printer fonts that come with your printer, Windows comes with a collection of *scalable* soft fonts, called TrueType fonts.

Most fonts appear on-screen almost exactly the way they print, but not all fonts that your printer can print can be displayed on-screen. If Windows does not have a screen font for a printer font, it substitutes a similar font. TrueType fonts print exactly as they look on-screen.

Note: *In Windows applications, you can easily distinguish the printer fonts from the TrueType fonts. In a font list box, the TrueType fonts are indicated with the words [TrueType] or a TT symbol.*

Adding Fonts

When you install a printer driver, screen fonts are installed automatically along with it. Screen fonts for cartridges and soft fonts are usually supplied on diskette by the vendor. If the vendor doesn't provide an installation program for installing screen fonts or if you purchase additional TrueType fonts for Windows, you can install the fonts by using the Control Panel Fonts option.

To install a font, follow these steps:

1. Double-click the Control Panel window.

2. Double-click the Fonts icon. The Fonts dialog box appears.

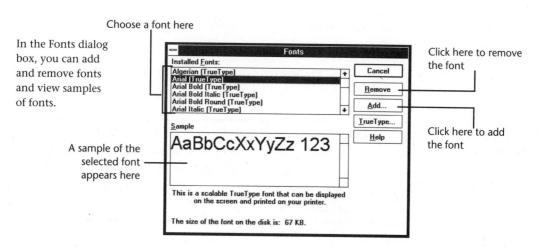

Choose a font here

In the Fonts dialog box, you can add and remove fonts and view samples of fonts.

Click here to remove the font

A sample of the selected font appears here

Click here to add the font

3. Click **A**dd. The Add fonts dialog box appears.

9

Choose the fonts
to add here

You can make
fonts available for
use in Windows in
the Add Fonts
dialog box.

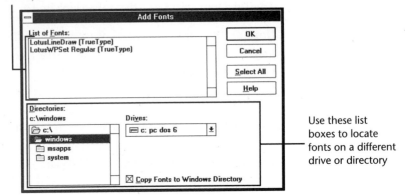

Use these list
boxes to locate
fonts on a different
drive or directory

4. From the **D**irectories and Dri**v**es lists, select the directory and drive that contain the fonts you want to add. If the fonts are on a diskette in drive A, for example, choose A from the Dri**v**es drop-down list.

5. From the List of **F**onts, select the fonts you want to add. To add all the fonts on the list, click **S**elect All.

6. Click OK to add the font or fonts. All added fonts appear in the Fonts dialog box.

7. Click Close to close the Fonts dialog box and return to the Control panel.

**If you have
problems...**

TrueType fonts require a great deal of memory. If your computer has a limited amount of available memory and your programs are running slowly or are having trouble loading, you can disable the TrueType fonts. To disable the TrueType fonts, choose **T**rueType in the Fonts dialog box, and deselect the **E**nable TrueType Fonts check box.

Chapter 10

Using IBM Tools

There are steps you can take to maintain your system and to keep your software and hardware secure. In this chapter, you learn to protect your system from computer viruses, to defragment your disks, to back up your data for safekeeping, and to undelete files that have been deleted accidentally.

Note: *Not all systems refer to the program group as IBM Tools.*

Protecting Your Computer from Viruses

Virus
A set of computer instructions hidden inside a program that can cause problems ranging from mischievous messages that appear on-screen to the destruction of your programs and data files.

One type of software problem that can harm your disks and cause serious data loss is a *virus*.

Viruses usually are found in free software distributed through electronic bulletin board systems (BBSs) and passed around on diskettes. Operators of bulletin board systems work very hard to avoid viruses, but the risk is not completely eliminated.

To avoid computer viruses, never use a program from someone you do not know. Before you use any program, talk with others who have used the program and make sure that they have had no problems. Also, make sure that the date and file size of both versions of the program are identical. Different file sizes on two supposed "copies" of the same program is a clue that the larger one might be infected with a virus.

Another way to help protect your system from viruses is to keep good, up-to-date backups available. Sometimes the only way to clean up an infected system is to restore it, using a virus-free backup. For more information on backing up data, see the section "Backing Up Your Data," later in this chapter.

Viruses are becoming all too common. Fortunately, there are antivirus protection programs you can use to detect and remove viruses from your computer.

PC DOS includes two versions of a powerful antivirus program: IBM AntiVirus/DOS and IBM AntiVirus/Windows. AntiVirus can prevent, detect, and remove computer viruses. The program can work in the background, automatically providing protection at all times, or you can use it to check selected diskettes and hard disks for viruses.

Starting AntiVirus/DOS

To start AntiVirus/DOS, follow these steps:

1. At the PC DOS command prompt, type **IBMAVD**.

2. Press **Enter**. The IBM AntiVirus/DOS screen appears.

AntiVirus/DOS uses a graphical user interface shell. You can use the keyboard or the mouse to make selections from menus or dialog boxes.

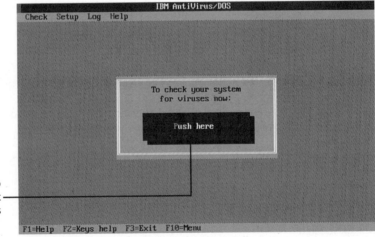

Click here to scan the current drive for viruses

Starting AntiVirus/Windows

To start IBM AntiVirus/Windows, follow these steps:

1. Start Windows.

2. Double-click the IBM Tools program group window. (For information on opening windows, see Chapter 4, "Making Windows Work."

3. Double-click the IBM AntiVirus icon. The IBM AntiVirus window opens.

The IBM AntiVirus/
Windows program
runs in a window
like other Windows
applications.

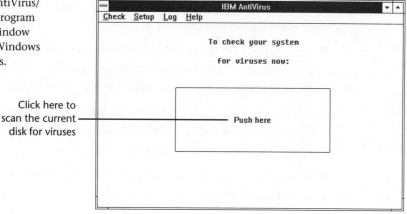

Click here to
scan the current
disk for viruses

Scanning for Viruses

In either program, follow these steps to scan the current disk for viruses:

1. Start the program as described above.

2. Choose Push Here to check the current drive. As AntiVirus scans a disk, it displays a status window showing you how much memory is being scanned and how many directories and files are being scanned.

3. To interrupt the scan, click the Stop button. A dialog box appears asking you to confirm that you want to cancel the scan.

4. Choose Yes to cancel the scan or choose No to continue the scan.

When the scan is complete, AntiVirus displays a status report of the viruses found.

Note: *If automated checking detects a virus, you are prompted to perform a thorough examination of your system in order to find every instance of the virus and to remove each one.*

5. Choose OK to return to the main AntiVirus screen.

6. Choose **C**heck, **E**xit to end the program.

The following list includes some of the other functions you can perform with IBM AntiVirus.

- To check a diskette or diskette drive other than the current drive, choose **C**heck, Check **d**iskettes.

- To automatically check your disks for viruses whenever you boot your system, choose **S**etup, **A**utomated check. You can choose to perform checks at every boot, daily, weekly, monthly, or no checks.

- To check PC DOS memory for viruses whenever you start PC DOS, choose **S**etup, **Sh**ield DOS. DOS Shielding disables viruses and prevents them from becoming active or spreading.

- To view information AntiVirus gathers during the current scan, choose **L**og, **C**urrent Log.

- To view the information gathered during the Previous scan, choose **L**og, **P**revious Log.

- To look at all the information gathered during every scan ever performed, choose **L**og, Cumulative **l**og.

- To display a list of Help topics choose **H**elp, **G**eneral help.

- To display a list of known viruses, choose **H**elp, Virus **l**ist.

Defragmenting Your Disks

Fragmented
Files that are stored in noncontiguous blocks around the disk.

Contiguous
Stored in adjacent memory blocks on disk.

Noncontiguous
Stored in memory blocks scattered around the disk.

Defragment
To remove disk fragmentation so that every file on the disk is in one contiguous block.

As you add to and delete files from a disk, the space available for new files is spread throughout the surface of the disk. When PC DOS writes a new file to a disk, PC DOS fills the first available space it comes to. If the file requires additional space, PC DOS uses the next available space as well.

In this way, files become split apart, or *fragmented*. They are no longer *contiguous*. Fragmented files lower disk performance; to read fragmented files, PC DOS must spend extra time seeking the data among the *noncontiguous* files.

PC DOS comes with a utility program, PC DOS Defragmenter, that you can use to *defragment* (or optimize) your disks for enhanced performance.

Note: *This utility is not found in the IBM Tools group. You access it from the PC DOS command prompt.*

You can tell how fragmented your disk is by using the CHKDSK command. To check your disk for fragmentation, type **CHKDSK *.*** at the PC DOS command prompt.

Type the command here

Use the CHKDSK
command to
display a status
report that
includes the
number of
noncontiguous
blocks containing
files on the
current disk.

```
C:\>CHKDSK *.*

Volume PC DOS 6     created 03-27-1994 11:23a
Volume Serial Number is 1C76-710D

   85,018,624 bytes total disk space
   12,652,544 bytes in 5 hidden files
      143,360 bytes in 56 directories
   69,085,184 bytes in 1,362 user files
    3,137,536 bytes available on disk

        2,048 bytes in each allocation unit
       41,513 total allocation units on disk
        1,532 available allocation units on disk

      655,360 total bytes memory
      553,632 bytes free

C:\COMMAND.COM Contains 2 non-contiguous blocks
C:\FILE0000.CHK Contains 2 non-contiguous blocks

C:\>
```

Check for
noncontiguous
blocks here

10

To optimize and defragment your disk, follow these steps:

1. At the PC DOS command prompt, type **DEFRAG**.

2. Press **Enter**. The main defragmenter screen appears.

The defragmenter
uses a graphical
user interface. You
can use a mouse to
select menu items
and commands,
or you can use a
keyboard.

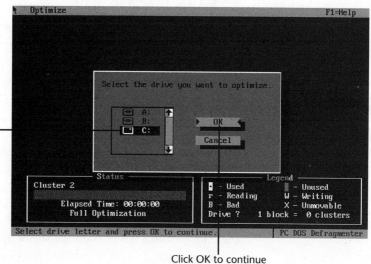

Choose a drive
to optimize and
defragment here

Click OK to continue

3. Choose the disk drive you want to defragment.

4. Choose OK. The Defragmenter analyzes the disk and makes a
recommendation for optimization.

5. Choose Optimize to proceed with the recommended optimization.

Note: *You can choose Configure to select a different method of optimization.*

During opti-
mization, the
defragmenter
displays a status
screen showing
you how blocks of
data are being
adjusted.

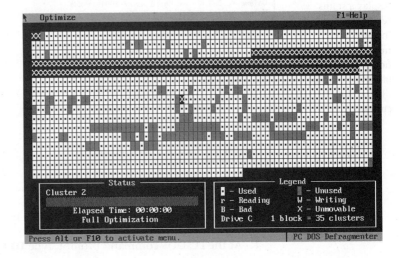

6. Choose OK in the Finished Condensing dialog box that appears when the optimization is complete.

7. Choose another drive to optimize, or choose **O**ptimize, **Ex**it to return to the PC DOS command prompt.

Backing Up Your Data

Backing up
To make a copy of
your data that can
be used in case the
original data is
accidentally dam-
aged or lost.

If you have ever experienced data loss, you know the value of *backing up* your data. Sudden power failures, software problems, mechanical fail-ures, and user mistakes can lead to the loss of valuable data. An up-to-date backup ensures that you can restore data quickly and resume working.

PC DOS comes with Central Point Backup, a program which provides protection against data loss by enabling you to make a backup copy of data. Central Point Backup can be used from the PC DOS command prompt or from Windows.

With Central Point Backup, you can choose any of the following methods:

■ *Full Backup.* Backs up all selected files.

- *Incremental Backup*. Backs up all files that have changed since the last full or incremental backup.

- *Differential Backup*. Backs up all files that have changed since the last full backup.

- *Unattended Backup*. Backs up your data to a tape, hard disk, or to a network volume at a time you specify.

Central Point Backup also includes utilities for comparing and verifying the backed-up data, and for restoring the backed-up data to its original source location.

Using Central Point Backup

The first time you start Central Point Backup, using either PC DOS or Windows, you are prompted to configure the program for your computer system. Configuring Central Point Backup saves certain information about your system in a Central Point Backup system file. Central Point Backup uses the information to perform reliable backups.

Configuring is automatic. All you have to do is to confirm the type of drives you have, and Central Point Backup does the rest. Simply follow the prompts that appear on-screen throughout the procedure. For more information, use the Help option in the Central Point Backup program.

The first time you start Central Point Backup from PC DOS, you are prompted to configure the program for your system.

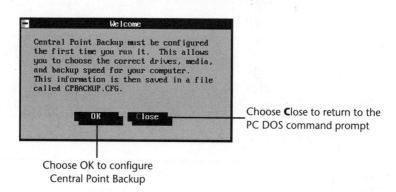

Choose **C**lose to return to the PC DOS command prompt

Choose OK to configure Central Point Backup

The first time you run Central Point Backup from Windows, you are prompted to configure it for your system.

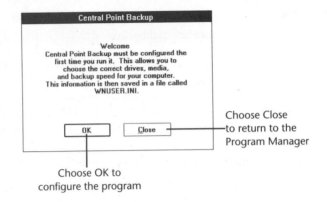

Choose Close to return to the Program Manager

Choose OK to configure the program

Using Central Point Backup for PC DOS

To start Central Point Backup for PC DOS, follow these steps:

1. At the PC DOS command prompt, type **CPBACKUP**. The Backup program starts and appears on-screen.

Central Point Backup for PC DOS uses a GUI. You can use the mouse or the keyboard to choose menu items and commands.

Click here to backup your files

Click here to restore backed-up files

Click here to compare backed-up files to original files

If you have problems...

If this is the first time you are using Central Point Backup, the Welcome screen prompts you to configure the program. Choose OK to begin the configuration, and then follow the instructions that appear on-screen.

---

2. Choose Backup. The Backup screen appears.

From the Central Point Backup screen, you can easily select the type of backup you want to perform, load setup files, and select the files you want to back up.

```
┌─┐                    Central Point Backup                    12:33p
│─│   File   Action   Options   Configure   Help
  ┌─┐                          Backup
  │─│
     ┌ Save Setup ┐ ┌ Verify ┐ ┌ Compress ┐ ┌ Reporting ┐ ┌ Scheduler ┐ ┌ Action ┐

        Setup:                          Backup From:
        ┌─────────────────────────┐     ┌───────────────────────┐ ┌─┐
        │ (No setup selected)   ▼ │     │ ▭ C:  PC DOS 6        │ │▲│
        └─────────────────────────┘     │                       │ └─┘
        Method:                         │                       │
        ┌─────────────────────────┐     │                       │
        │ Full                  ▼ │     │                       │ ┌─┐
        └─────────────────────────┘     └───────────────────────┘ └▼┘
        ┌────────────────────────────┐      Select Files for Backup  ▪
        │ 0 drives                   │   Backup To:   ▼
        │ 0 directories              │   ┌───────────────────────┐
        │ 0 files                    │   │ ▭ A: 360kb  (5-1/4)  ▼│
        │ 0 bytes         0 disks    │   └───────────────────────┘
        │            00:00 minutes   │
        └────────────────────────────┘          ┌ Start Backup ┐

  Load a pre-defined backup/restore setup file
```

Click here to choose a setup file

Click here to choose a backup method

Click here to start the backup

Click here to choose a destination drive

Click here to choose files to back up

3. Choose the options you want to use for the backup. Choose a setup file or choose the specific method to use, for example, and select the files you want to back up. For more information, consult on-line Help for this utility.

4. Choose **S**tart Backup to begin backing up.

Using Central Point Backup for Windows

To start Central Point Backup for Windows, follow these steps:

1. Start Windows.

2. Double-click the IBM Tools group window. For information on opening windows, see Chapter 4, "Making Windows Work."

3. Double-click the Central Point Backup icon. The Central Point Backup program starts, and the Central Point Backup Main Menu window appears on-screen.

If you have problems...

If this is the first time you are using Central Point Backup, the Welcome screen prompts you to configure the program. Choose OK to begin the configuration, and then follow the instructions that appear on-screen.

Choose Backup here

From the Central
Point Backup Main
Menu window,
you can choose to
back up, restore, or
compare data.

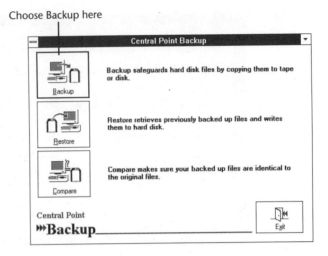

4. Choose Backup to display the Central Point Backup program
window.

Click here to choose a built-in setup file

With Central
Point Backup you
can easily select
the type of backup
you want to
perform, and the
files or directories
you want to
back up.

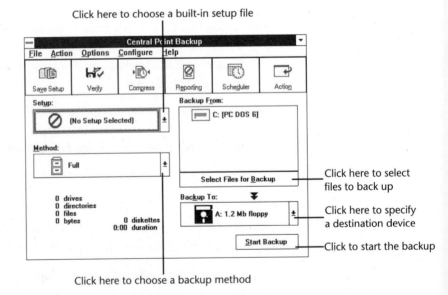

Click here to select
files to back up

Click here to specify
a destination device

Click to start the backup

Click here to choose a backup method

5. Choose the options you want to use for the backup. Choose a setup
file or choose the specific method to use, for example, and select
the files you want to back up. For more information, consult on-
line Help for this utility.

6. Choose **S**tart Backup to begin backing up.

Understanding Backup Strategies

The key to an effective backup strategy is scheduling. You must determine how frequently you need to back up to ensure a minimal amount of data loss in case of a catastrophe. How often you should back up and the type of backup you should use depend in large part on how frequently your data changes.

Consider the following questions:

- How valuable are my files to me or my business?

- How many of my files change on a daily basis?

- How long would it take to replace those files if something happened to them?

With this information, you can determine the backup strategy that best suits your needs.

When you develop a backup strategy, follow these general guidelines:

Backup media

The storage media on which you store the backed up data.

- Alternate between two sets of *backup media* (usually disks or tape, or a combination of the two) so that you are never overwriting your last backup with the current backup.

- Schedule a set time each day for backing up. Schedule weekly backups on Fridays and daily backups on Mondays through Thursdays.

No matter what type of media you use to back up, you can use two of Central Point Backup's built-in setup files to make sure that your backup data is always current.

- The weekly setup file is set to back up all files on your first hard disk (usually C).

- The daily setup file backs up only the changed files since the last full or incremental backup.

Diskette Backup Strategies

To back up all files to diskettes on a weekly basis, follow these steps:

1. At the scheduled weekly backup time on Friday, start Central Point Backup from the PC DOS command prompt by typing **CPBACKUP WEEKLY**.

2. Begin your backup, using the first set of diskettes.

3. Label each diskette with its backup sequence number, name, and set number. For example, label the first diskette #1, Friday backup, Set A. The next diskette would be #2, Friday backup, Set A, and so on.

To back up only changed files on a daily basis, follow these steps:

1. At the scheduled backup time, start Central Point Backup from the PC DOS command prompt by typing **CPBACKUP DAILY**.

2. Insert the backup diskettes as prompted.

3. Label each diskette with its proper sequence number (#1 of Set A, #2 of Set A, and so on).

For many people, a monthly full backup is sufficient when coupled with daily backups of the changed files.

Everyone should use one of the following daily methods, depending on particular needs:

■ Do a daily differential backup to diskettes. Alternate between two sets of disks for safety. When the sets use more than six diskettes, do another full backup. The differential method does not save multiple daily versions of the changed files. It saves only the latest versions.

■ Do a separate incremental backup on Monday (which starts a new backup set), followed by daily incremental backups to diskettes. This keeps daily versions of the files that change but creates less backup sets than using separate incremental backups exclusively.

Tape Backup Strategies

While your computer system probably did not come with a tape backup system, you may want to consider adding one. A tremendous advantage to using a tape drive is that it automates the backup procedure. One simple strategy is to use at least two tapes so that you are never writing over your last backup with the current backup. You can use Central Point Backup's built-in weekly and daily setup files to facilitate a two-tape backup strategy.

10

To back up data using the two-tape strategy, follow these steps:

1. Schedule a weekly full backup, using the WEEKLY setup file and tape #1.

2. Schedule a daily backup using the DAILY setup file and tape #1.

3. Use tape #2 the second week, and continue alternating tapes each week.

Undeleting Files and Directories

PC DOS comes with the Central Point Undelete program (Undelete), which you can use to recover most files and directories that have been deleted using the DELETE command.

Undelete is automatically installed when you install PC DOS. You can also choose to install a version of Undelete for Windows.

Undelete can undelete most files, but it is most effective when you protect files with one of the following methods of deletion protection:

DOS

Delete Sentry

Delete Tracker

Novell NetWare 386

DR DOS DelWatch

Note: *For more information about these deletion-protection methods, see the section "Understanding Deletion-Protection Methods," later in this chapter.*

In any case, you should always undelete files as soon as possible after the deletion to maximize your chances of recovering all your data.

If you have problems...   If you have accidentally erased or formatted your entire disk, use UNFORMAT to recover the disk.

Starting Undelete

Undelete works in conjunction with Data Monitor, a memory-resident program that includes several options to guard against data loss and protect important data.

You can use Undelete in any of three ways:

- The Windows method enables you to manage your deleted files in the Windows environment.

- The PC DOS command-line method of Undelete is a simplified program that prompts you file by file through the files it can undelete.

- The full-screen PC DOS method uses a graphical user interface to help you locate and recover files.

Starting the Windows Version of Undelete

To start the Windows version of Undelete, follow these steps:

1. Start Windows.

2. Double-click the IBM Tools group window. (For information on opening windows, see Chapter 4, "Making Windows Work.")

3. Double-click the Undelete icon.

Click here to display the contents of a different directory

Click here to sort the file list

In the Windows version of Undelete, you can easily undelete files, display the deleted contents of directories, find files, and sort files—all in the Windows environment.

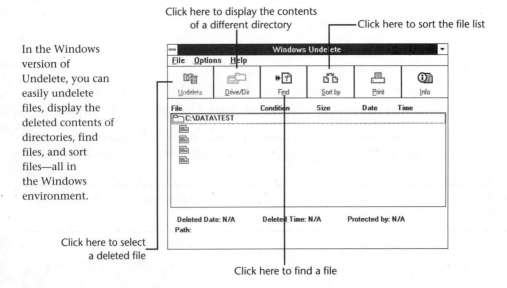

Click here to select a deleted file

Click here to find a file

Starting the Command-Line Version of Undelete

To use the command-line version of Undelete, follow these steps:

1. At the PC DOS command prompt, type
UNDELETE *drive:\directory\filename.ext*.

2. Press **Enter**. For each occurrence of a deleted file, PC DOS displays
a prompt asking if you want to recover the file.

3. To recover the file press, **Y**. To leave the file deleted, press **N**.

4. When prompted, enter the first letter of the file name.

Type the command here

You can specify
which files you
want to recover
using the
command-line
version of
Undelete.

Respond to the prompts

```
C:\DATA\TEST>UNDELETE *.*

Undelete V8 (c)1990-1992 Central Point Software, Inc.

Directory: C:\DATA\TEST
?AXES    .DOC      23552 03/17/94 10:51a    Poor
Do you want to recover this file? (Y/N)N

?ENEFITS.DOC       2560 08/24/93  7:55p Destroyed
Do you want to recover this file? (Y/N)N

?OJILL   .DOC      12288 03/06/94  9:35p Destroyed
Do you want to recover this file? (Y/N)N

?UDGET   .DOC       2048 10/07/93  2:26p Destroyed
Do you want to recover this file? (Y/N)N


C:\DATA\TEST>
```

You can find out which files have been deleted by using the /LIST
parameter with the UNDELETE command.

To display a list of deleted files, along with the deletion protection
method being used, type **UNDELETE /LIST** at the PC DOS command
prompt. PC DOS displays a list of deleted files for the current directory.

Starting the Full-Screen Version of Undelete

The full-screen version of Undelete has a graphical user interface. You
can use a mouse to choose menu items and commands, or you can use a
keyboard.

To start the full-screen version of Undelete, follow these steps:

1. At the PC DOS command prompt, type **UNDELETE**.

2. Press **Enter**. The Undelete program appears on-screen.

You can use a mouse to choose commands in the full-screen PC DOS version of Undelete.

The Directory Tree area

The File List area

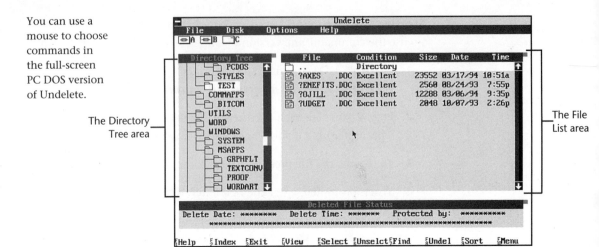

Using the Full-Screen Version of Undelete

When the Undelete window appears, the Directory Tree area on the left shows the directory structure of the selected drive. The File List area on the right shows subdirectories and files that have been deleted from the highlighted directory.

You can use a mouse in Undelete, or you can use function keys. Some of the available functions keys are described in Table 10.1.

Table 10.1 Undelete Function Keys

Function Key	Description
F1	Provides on-line Help about the selected item
F2	Displays the Help index
F3	Exits to the PC DOS command prompt
F4	Displays the contents of the highlighted file
F5	Enables you to select files by file name specification
F6	Enables you to deselect files by file name specification
F7	Opens the Find Deleted Files window
F8	Undeletes the selected file or files
F9	Enables you to specify a sort order for listing files
F10	Activates the horizontal menu bar

Understanding the Condition of a Deleted File

Cluster

A unit of disk space where files are stored.

The condition of each deleted file appears next to the file name in the File List area. The condition indicates how completely Undelete can recover the deleted file. Undelete assigns conditions based on the status of the file's *clusters*.

Table 10.2 describes the different file conditions assigned by Undelete.

Table 10.2 Undelete File Conditions	
Condition	**What You Can Expect to Recover**
Perfect	You can undelete the file completely and automatically.
Excellent	All the file's clusters are available and unfragmented and can be undeleted automatically. There is a slight chance that some data may not be available.
Good	One or more of the file's clusters are in use by another file and are not available. Some data may have been overwritten.
Poor	The file's first cluster, and possibly additional clusters, are not available. You may be able to use advanced delete methods to recover the data.
Destroyed	The file cannot be undeleted because all its known clusters are in use by other files. You may be able to use advanced delete methods to recover the data.
None	The file cannot be undeleted because it had no data in it when it was deleted.
Existing	The file has not been deleted.
Lost file	The file was found by scanning for lost files. It is a deleted file whose directory has probably been deleted.
Recovered	The file was undeleted during the current session.
Purged	The file was purged from a deletion-protection directory during the current session. It cannot be recovered.

Understanding Deletion-Protection Methods

The Deleted File Status panel indicates what method of deletion protection was being used when the highlighted file was deleted. Table 10.3 describes the different deletion-protection methods.

Table 10.3 Deletion-Protection Methods

Protection Method	Description
Delete Sentry	Files protected by the Delete Sentry method can be undeleted in perfect condition because they are saved in a hidden directory.
Delete Tracker	PC DOS leaves files protected by the Delete Tracker method on the disk but marks the file's clusters as available. As long as the file's clusters have not been overwritten by new data, the file can be recovered in excellent condition.
DOS	Indicates that no deletion-protection method was used. Files are undeleted based on their entries in the DOS directory and in the File Allocation Table on the disk.
NetWare	Indicates that Novell NetWare's method of deletion protection was used on a network drive. The files can be undeleted in perfect condition because they actually remain on the drive until they are purged or the space they occupied is overwritten.
DelWatch	Indicates that the DR DOS method of deletion protection was used. Files can be undeleted in perfect condition.

Sorting the File List

By default, Undelete sorts by file name. However, you can change the order in which Undelete displays files by selecting a different sort order. For example, you might want all the BAT files or all the files created on a certain date listed together so that you can quickly find the one you want to undelete. Or, if you know that the file is very small, you might sort the list in order of size.

If you select more than one file to undelete, the sort order determines the order in which the files will be undeleted. Before you simultaneously undelete a group of files that have different conditions, sort them in order of condition so that Undelete can recover the files that are in the best condition first. The condition of a file can change as the files preceding it are undeleted.

To change the sort order, follow these steps:

1. Choose **O**ptions, **S**ort By. The Sort by dialog box appears.

In the Sort By
dialog box, you
can change the
sort order to
more effectively
undelete deleted
files.

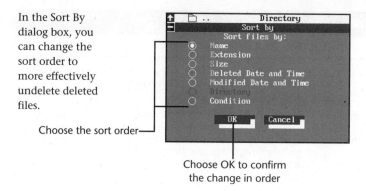

Choose the sort order——

Choose OK to confirm
the change in order

2. Choose one of the following sort orders:

■ **N**ame. Sorts the files by file name.

■ **E**xtension. Sorts the files by file extension.

■ **S**ize. Sorts the files by size, with the smallest files first.

■ **D**eleted Date and Time. Sorts files protected by Delete Sentry and Delete Tracker by the date that files were deleted. Within each date group, files are sorted in order of time deleted. DOS-deleted files that have an unknown date are listed last in unchanged order.

■ **M**odified Date and Time. Sorts the files in order of the date that files were last modified. Within each date group, files are sorted in order of time last modified.

■ Di**r**ectory. Sorts the files alphabetically by directory name. This option is available only in the expanded file list displayed for network drives and files found by specification, where the directory tree is not shown.

■ Condi**t**ion. Sorts the files by condition in the following order: Perfect, Excellent, Good, Poor, Destroyed, Existing.

3. Choose OK.

Selecting Files

You must select the files that you want to undelete. Table 10.4 describes the methods you can use to select files.

Table 10.4 Methods of Selecting Files	
To:	**Do This:**
Select one file	Use the mouse or the arrow keys to highlight the file you want to select and click the left mouse button, press **Enter**, or press the spacebar.
Select or deselect a group of files with the mouse	Press and hold down the right mouse button. Use the mouse or the arrow keys to highlight the first file you want to select; then press and hold down the left mouse button. Drag the mouse to the last file you want to select. Release both mouse buttons.
Select a group of files by specification	Choose **O**ptions, Select **b**y Name. Enter a file specification and choose OK.
Deselect a group of files by specification	Choose **O**ptions, **U**nselect by Name. Enter a file specification and choose OK.

Undeleting a File

To undelete a file in perfect or excellent condition, follow these steps:

1. Select the file in the File List area.

2. Press **F8**. The file is undeleted and stored in its original directory.

To undelete a file in good condition, follow these steps:

1. Select the file in the File List area.

2. Choose **F**ile, Undelete **T**o. The Drive Selection dialog box appears.

3. Select the disk drive in which to store the recovered file.

4. Choose OK. The Undelete To dialog box appears.

5. Specify a path in which to store the file.

6. Choose OK. Undelete recovers the file.

Note: *Undeleting a file to a different drive is useful as a safety precaution, no matter what condition the deleted file is in. This action leaves the original deleted file unchanged but restores a copy of the file to the specified drive and directory.*

If you have problems...	If the file you want to delete is in any condition other than perfect, excellent, or good, you probably need to use advanced methods to recover the data.

Renaming an Existing File

Existing file
A file that has not been deleted.

If the file you are undeleting has the same name as an *existing file*, Undelete prompts you to change the existing file name. This may happen if the deleted file is a previous version of an existing file. You can rename the existing file before you undelete the deleted one and thereby keep both files in the same directory.

To rename an existing file using Undelete, follow these steps:

1. In the Directory Tree area, choose the directory that contains the file you want to rename.

2. Choose **O**ptions, **Sh**ow Existing Files to display existing files in the File List area along with deleted files.

3. In the File List area, select the existing file you want to rename.

4. Choose **F**ile, **A**dvanced Undelete, **R**ename Existing File. The Rename Existing File dialog box appears.

5. Type a new name for the existing file.

6. Choose **R**ename.

Note: *To remove the existing files from the file list, select **O**ptions, **Sh**ow Existing Files again.*

Undeleting Files on a Network

If you are undeleting files on a network drive, Undelete lists the deleted files that were protected by Delete Sentry or Novell NetWare 386 method of deletion protection. In place of a directory tree, Undelete shows the deleted files' paths in an expanded file list.

If a network directory is hidden, Undelete will not display the files unless the directory's hidden attribute is changed. Also, if you are using Delete Sentry, files deleted by other users do not appear in the list. The Novell NetWare method of deletion protection shows all files; you can undelete files that you have deleted with your current user name.

If you use Novell NetWare's method of deletion protection to protect the network drive, users can see deleted files but cannot recover files unless the network administrator has assigned Create rights to the directory that contained the deleted files.

If none of these methods of deletion protection were used on the network drive, Undelete does not list any deleted files.

The following commands are not available if you are undeleting files on a network drive:

File, Tree & File List

File, Advanced Undelete

All commands on the disk menu

Options, Show Existing Files

Options, Use Mirror File

Note: *NetWare does not keep track of deleted directories, but the program does track the files in deleted directories.*

Undeleting Directories and Their Files

A directory contains file entries identifying the names, starting locations, and other information for all files that belong to it. When you delete a directory, deleted files that were in that directory no longer appear in Undelete's file lists. However, the deleted directory appears, identified with a folder icon and <dir> listed as the file size.

As soon as you undelete a directory, any deleted files it contained appear in Undelete's file lists. If you cannot find a deleted file, try to locate its directory by using the Directory Tree and File List area. When you undelete the directory, it appears in the Directory Tree. Select that directory, and then select and undelete any of its deleted files.

If you cannot find a deleted file's directory, you can still find the file or its data by using one of Undelete's disk scan methods. For information on scanning disks for lost files, refer to on-line Help for more information.

To undelete a directory, follow these steps:

1. Select the directory in the Directory Tree area.

2. Press **F8**.

3. If Undelete cannot determine the location of all the parts of the directory, it displays the Directory Undelete dialog box.

   In the Directory Undelete dialog box, you must identify the groups of file entries that belong in the directory you are undeleting.

   Note: *In the Directory Undelete dialog box, you do not select individual files to undelete. You decide whether the entire group of file entries displayed in the list box represents files that belong in the directory you want to undelete.*

4. In the Directory Undelete dialog box, take one of the following actions:

   ■ If the group of file entries displayed in the File List area was in the directory, select **A**dd.

   ■ If the group of file entries displayed in the File List area was not in the directory, select **S**kip.

5. Undelete searches for the next probable group of files and displays it in the File List area. Repeat step 4 until the entire directory has been recovered.

Note: *Choose Undelete in the Directory Undelete dialog box to recover the directory without selecting all the file groups. Undelete does its best to recover as much of the directory as possible.*

Finding Deleted Files

You can search for deleted files by entering a file specification. This is useful if you cannot find a deleted file in the File List area or when you want to display all deleted files on the disk in one listing.

To specify deleted files, follow these steps:

1. Select the drive that contained the deleted file.

2. Choose **F**ile, **F**ind Deleted Files. The Find Deleted Files dialog box appears.

You can search a disk for specified deleted files.

Enter a file specification here

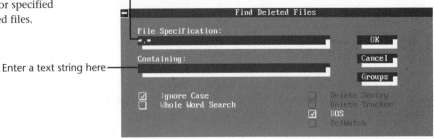

Enter a text string here

3. Complete one or more of the following actions:

- ■ In the File Specification text box, type the file specification for the file or files you want to find. You can use PC DOS wild-card characters.

- ■ In the Containing text box, enter a *text string* that you know is contained in the deleted file you want to find.

Text string
A series of text characters, including words and numbers,

- ■ Choose **G**roups to find files associated with a particular application program.

4. Select one or more of the text search options:

- ■ Choose **I**gnore Case to find files containing the text— whether it is uppercase or lowercase.

- ■ Choose **W**hole Word to find the text only if it is entered in complete words.

5. Select the deletion-protection methods for which to search.

If you have problems...

If the Delete Sentry, Delete Tracker, or DelWatch options are dimmed, no files on the current drive are protected by these methods.

---

6. Choose OK. Undelete displays all files that match the specifications in an expanded file list in the Find Deleted Files window.

7. To return to the Directory Tree and File List areas, choose **F**ile, Tree & **F**ile List.

Scanning the Disk for Lost Files and Deleted Data

If you have not found a deleted file using any of the previous methods, you can scan the entire disk for lost files or for deleted data that is not associated with any file or directory.

To scan the disk for lost deleted files, follow these steps:

1. Select the directory in which you want lost files to be recovered. Undelete recovers lost files to the current directory.

2. Select **D**isk, Scan for **L**ost Deleted Files. The Scan for Lost Files dialog box appears.

You can scan a disk to try to find deleted files that are no longer associated with a directory.

3. Select the deletion-protection methods for which to scan.

If you have problems...   If no files on the current drive are protected by Delete Sentry or Delete Tracker, that check box is dimmed and you cannot select it.

---

4. Select OK. Undelete scans the disk for files protected by the method or methods you selected.

When the disk scan is complete, the list of files found appears in the Find Deleted Files dialog box, with Lost File as each file's condition. Lost files retain their original names and other information, so you can easily select and undelete the files you want.

Scanning Free Clusters for Deleted Data

You can scan the disk's free clusters—disk space no longer associated with any existing file or directory—for a specified type of data or a text string.

Note: *When scanning the disk's free clusters, Undelete does not look at files protected by Delete Sentry or DelWatch.*

To scan free clusters for deleted data, follow these steps:

1. Select the directory in which you want clusters containing the specified type of data to be recovered. Undelete recovers clusters to the current directory.

2. Choose one of the following:

   ■ **D**isk, Scan for **D**ata Types, to select the type of data to scan for (Lotus 1-2-3 and Symphony, dBASE, or normal text).

   ■ **D**isk, Scan for **C**ontents, to specify a word, phrase, or text string for which to scan. It does not matter whether you use uppercase or lowercase letters.

3. Choose OK.

When Undelete finds a contiguous group of free clusters that match the information you specified, it counts the group as a file and gives it a unique name. Undelete tries to match lost data with directory entries, making its best guess at the file name. When the disk scan is complete, the list of clusters found appears in the Find Deleted Files window.

Using PenDOS

Pen-based
Application programs designed for use with a tablet or digitizer pen input device.

PC DOS comes with PenDOS, a utility program that enables you to use *pen-based* application programs as well as standard mouse-based PC DOS application programs on any 386 or higher computer. Pen-based application programs make computing easier than ever; you can write, draw, and issue commands simply by pointing and using a pen.

PenDOS enables you to use the mouse as a pen. You do not need any other special equipment to compute with a pen.

Tablet
A peripheral device that enables you to input information into a computer by writing on it with a pen device.

Using a pen *tablet* computer or externally attached digitizer tablet, you can write naturally because PenDOS includes CIC's Handwriter Recognition System. As an introduction to computing with a pen, this version of Handwriter recognizes numbers and symbols only. A full version of Handwriter that recognizes uppercase and lowercase letters, numbers, punctuation marks, and symbols is available separately from IBM.

Preparing Your System for PenDOS

You can install PenDOS on your system during PC DOS setup and installation.

Before starting PenDOS, make sure that you have the proper hardware installed and the correct tablet driver selected. If you have a pen tablet computer with a self-contained digitizer, you should have chosen that computer's tablet driver when you set up PC DOS.

If you have an externally attached digitizer, make sure that the digitizer is connected to the proper communication port on your computer. Refer to the digitizer manufacturer's instructions for the proper installation procedure. You should have also selected the proper tablet driver for your digitizer during PC DOS Setup. If you will be using your mouse as your pointing device, select the Digitizing Pad Emulation via Mouse tablet driver during PC DOS Setup.

The PC DOS Setup program modifies your CONFIG.SYS file by adding the appropriate device statement when you select PenDOS as an optional tool and then select a tablet or mouse device.

Starting PenDOS

You can modify your AUTOEXEC.BAT to have PenDOS start automatically whenever you start your computer, or you can type the PENDOS command at the PC DOS command prompt each time you want to start PenDOS.

To start PenDOS, follow these steps:

1. At the PC DOS command prompt, type **PENDOS**.

2. Press **Enter**.

Understanding Phoenix PCMCIA Support

PC DOS provides support for the computers with slots conforming to the Personal Computer Memory Card International Association (PCMCIA) standard.

PC Cards

Credit card-sized devices that attach PCMCIS sockets inside the PC. They are used to attach peripherals such as memory-expansion cards, faxes, and modems.

The PCMCIA standard allows for the uniform development of *PC Cards*, credit card-sized devices, for portable, laptop, some desktop, and palmtop computer accessories, such as memory-expansion cards, fax and modem attachments, and interfaces to corporate networks. A computer having PCMCIA support provides sockets into which you can insert PC Cards. PC Cards enable you to extend the capabilities of your computer by adding functions, such as the following:

- Communications (modems, Token-Ring, EtherNet, 3270, and 5250)

- Memory (DRAM, SRAM, and EPROM)

- Rotating media (ATA disk drives)

- Solid state disk drives

The PCMCIA standard defines both the hardware and software interfaces for PCMCIA sockets and cards. The Card Services module is the operating system software layer for PCMCIA and defines a set of application programming interfaces (APIs) that system and application software can use to communicate with PCMCIA sockets and cards.

Using PC Cards

The PCMCIA sockets are numbered 1 through *n* where *n* is the number of sockets on your system. You insert a PC Card by aligning it with a PCMCIA socket and sliding the card into the socket. You remove a card by pressing the eject button (or by some other ejection means provided by your system vendor) on the PCMCIA socket to eject the card.

After the PC Cards are installed and operating, you can interchange PCMCIA PC Cards in the PCMCIA PC Card slots (adhering to certain precautions) with little or no knowledge of the technology involved in the inner workings of the software. This capability to easily insert and remove PC Cards enables you to move devices and data from one computer to another.

Preparing Your Computer for Use with PCMCIA Devices

If you have a notebook, laptop, palmtop, or desktop personal computer, you can take full advantage of many of the functions of PCMCIA Support software. Using Phoenix PCMCIA Support, the installation and operation of PCMCIA devices will seem almost transparent.

In order to install, modify, and maintain PCMCIA Support software, however, you must have an understanding of PC DOS, Windows, and the ability to modify the CONFIG.SYS and SYSTEM.INI files that are necessary for adaptation or modification of the many drivers and utilities that are managed by PCMCIA Support. Drivers are ordinarily included in either CONFIG.SYS (PC DOS drivers) or SYSTEM.INI (Windows drivers).

Both PC DOS and Windows executable files can reside on any disk to which the system has access. You can locate the PC DOS drivers on any drive; however, you must specify the full path for PC DOS drivers in the CONFIG.SYS file. For PC DOS to find and process a file, the EXE or COM file must reside in the current directory, or in a directory specified using the PATH command in the AUTOEXEC.BAT file, or it must be typed in the CONFIG.SYS file, using the full path name. For more information, see Chapter 8, "Configuring Your Personal Computer."

Windows drivers must reside in the \WINDOWS\SYSTEM directory. You can run Windows executable files from any directory if you specify the full path when you run the program or when you create or define a Windows icon. For more information, see Chapter 4, "Making Windows Work."

The Phoenix PCMCIA components must be loaded for you to have PCMCIA Support available. These components can be loaded in any of the following manners:

- As a device driver in your CONFIG.SYS, with either the default options or modified options.

- As a terminate-and-stay-resident (TSR) program.

Note: *For information on adding device driver statements in the CONFIG.SYS file or starting TSR programs, consult Chapter 8, "Configuring Your Personal Computer."*

Using the MSCDEX Command

CD-ROM
An acronym for
compact-disk, read-
only memory. CD-
ROMs are storage
devices that can be
read using CD-ROM
drives.

PC DOS 6.3 provides support for *CD-ROM* drives. You can use the
MSCDEX command to access and control CD-ROM drives attached to
your computer.

To use the MSCDEX command to access CD-ROM drives, you must
first load the device driver that came with your CD-ROM into the
CONFIG.SYS file. For more information, see Chapter 8, "Configuring
Your Personal Computer," and the CD-ROM drive documentation.

After you have the device drivers included in your CONFIG.SYS file, you
can use the MSCDEX command from the PC DOS command prompt by
typing **MSCDEX** and specifying the device driver. You can also add the
MSCDEX command to your AUTOEXEC.BAT file so that the command
is enabled every time you start your computer. For more information
about adding commands to the AUTOEXEC.BAT file, see Chapter 8,
"Configuring Your Personal Computer."

To add the MSCDEX command to your AUTOEXEC.BAT file, the command statement must include a /D:*drivename* parameter that matches
the /D:*drivename* parameter used in the CONFIG.SYS file for the CD-
ROM device driver. Each CD-ROM device driver currently in use must
have a unique driver name.

Note: *The device driver for your CD-ROM comes with your CD-ROM, not with
PC DOS. To use MSCDEX.EXE in PC DOS to access and use your CD-ROM,
the CD-ROM device driver must be loaded in the CONFIG.SYS file.*

Chapter 11

Using Data Compression

Data compression
The process of reducing the number of bytes required to represent data so that the data consumes less disk space.

It seems that no matter how much disk space you have when you first get a computer, you soon need more. Windows and Windows applications are generally large programs that require large amounts of disk space to run on a computer.

When you run out of disk space, you have a few options:

- You can delete some of your data.

- You can buy another disk.

- You can compress your data so that more fits into the same amount of space.

Caution
Compression is a feature that only knowledgeable users should attempt. This chapter is just an overview of data compression.

Data compression is accomplished by using a data compression software utility. PC DOS comes with a data compression utility, SuperStor/DS.

In this chapter, you learn what data compression is and what it can do for your computer. In addition, you learn about using SuperStor/DS.

Understanding Data Compression

Byte
A measurement of information stored on a disk. One byte is equal to approximately one character.

The amount of data that can fit on a storage disk is measured in bytes—one *byte* equals approximately one character. Every disk holds a specific number of bytes. When the disk is full, you cannot store even a single additional byte on it. (See Chapter 1, "Understanding System Basics," for more information about disks and disk capacities.)

By using data compression techniques, you can compress your data so that you can store more on your disk.

Basically, data compression replaces repetitive data bytes or characters with fewer, specially encoded bytes. This compression is based on the idea that identical strings of bytes or characters consistently appear in your files. The data compression program assigns a shorter code to these strings. Whenever the strings appear in the data, the compression program substitutes the shorter code.

This process reduces the amount of data that must be coded on disk. The amount of the reduction depends on how long the original string of bytes is and how short the code substituting for the string is.

If the string of bytes is the word *the* and the shortened code replaces *the* with a percent sign (%) each time that string of bytes appears, for example, you get a 3:1 compression ratio because you are substituting three letters (*t*, *h*, and *e*) for one symbol (%).

Compressed volume file

A compressed disk where the compressed data is stored.

When you prepare a disk for compression, you create a *compressed volume file* (CVF) where the compressed data is stored.

When you read the data from the disk, the disk compression program accesses the CVF to read the data and then replaces the shortened code with the original data string.

Some types of files can be compressed using much higher compression ratios than other files. Because most people have a variety of file types on their disks, SuperStor/DS uses a standard compression ratio of 2:1. However, you can specify a higher compression ratio. For example, if most of your files are graphics files, you may want to specify a ratio as high as 8:1.

The compression ratio does not affect the degree to which SuperStor/DS can compress your files; the ratio affects the size of the CVF table that SuperStor/DS creates. The larger the CVF, the more data it can hold.

Use the following table to determine the optimum compression ratio for a disk:

Table 11.1 Compression Ratios	
File Type	**Range of Possible Ratios**
Executable programs	1.4:1 to 2:1
Word processing documents	2:1 to 4:1
Text files	2:1 to 8:1
Database files	2:1 to 8:1
Spreadsheet files	2:1 to 4:1
Video image files	2:1 to 8:1
CAD/CAM files	3:1 to 8:1

11

Determining If You Need Data Compression

Data compression programs provide the means of increasing your disk storage capacity. SuperStor/DS and other compression programs effectively double the disk capacity without changing the data.

After installing a data compression program such as SuperStor/DS, you use your programs and files the same way you used them before they were compressed—except that they take approximately half the space they used to take on your disk.

Following are some reasons you might want to use a data compression program.

- You do not have enough space on your desktop computer's hard disk to install new application programs or utilities.

- When you try to store a file, you receive one of these messages: `Not Enough Disk Space` or `Disk Full`.

- Your laptop or notebook does not have enough storage space to load and run all the programs you require.

- You do not want to invest in upgrading your equipment only because your hard disk is not large enough.

- You want to store more data on one diskette.

Understanding SuperStor/DS

PC DOS comes with the SuperStor/DS data compression program. Some advantages in using SuperStor/DS include the following:

■ *DOS operating system commands have been enhanced for use with SuperStor/DS*. Certain DOS utilities and system files have been enhanced to support the SuperStor/DS data compression program, including FORMAT, CHKDSK, and SYS.

■ *The program is transparent to DOS and application programs*. You continue to use your applications and files as you did before you installed SuperStor/DS. Your compressed files are automatically uncompressed when you read them and compressed again when you write to them.

■ *You do not need any additional hardware*. No add-in boards are required, and you do not need to set jumpers and switches to have the benefits of data compression. Expansion slots are left free for other uses.

■ *All media types are supported. SuperStor/DS extends the benefits of compression to all types of hard disks and diskettes*.

Mount
To make available for use—a term applied to disks and disk drives.

■ *The SuperStor/DS driver automatically mounts (automounts) all logical drives with removable media on start-up*. When a diskette is inserted into a drive, SuperStor/DS recognizes whether the diskette is a normal noncompressed diskette or a SuperStor/DS automount diskette.

■ *Compressed disks can be read and written by other systems.* SuperStor/DS provides a special Universal Data Exchange (UDE) driver that allows compressed data on diskettes to be read by systems that do not have SuperStor/DS installed.

■ *Compression can be applied to all or only part of a disk*. Because SuperStor/DS has a flexible configuration, you can compress your entire disk or compress only the free space.

■ *You can specify the optimum compression ratio for your files*. You do not have to use the standard compression ratio of 2:1 for files that are more easily compressed, such as graphics program files.

■ ***Data integrity is safeguarded***. You cannot restart (reboot) your computer during critical operations. The disk is set to read-only status when an error is detected. You cannot write data until you run the REPAIR DISK utility to correct the error.

■ ***You can use the DOS interface to access the SuperStor/DS utilities***. Just type the SuperStor/DS commands from the PC DOS command prompt.

11

Starting SuperStor/DS

The files required for you to start SuperStor/DS are loaded onto your system during the installation and setup of PC DOS.

Following are some guidelines for preparing your system for data compression. Many factors could potentially cause damage to your data and your hardware if you do not prepare adequately for data compression.

Hardware and Software Requirements

To use SuperStor/DS, your system must meet the following requirements:

■ The operating system must be PC DOS 6.1 or higher.

■ You must have an IBM-compatible computer with at least 512K of available memory after PC DOS is started. (Use the CHKDSK command to verify this amount by looking at the number of bytes free.)

■ You must have at least one 5 1/4-inch or one 3 1/2-inch diskette drive.

■ You must have a hard disk of any size with at least 4M of free space on the start-up (boot) drive or 2M free on nonboot drives.

■ SuperStor/DS requires 40K of conventional memory to run.

■ You can have a partition larger than 256M; however, you can compress only the first 256M of the drive.

■ You can use SuperStor/DS with Windows 3.1.

■ You cannot use SuperStor/DS to compress data on a partition that contains any OS/2 files. If you compress a partition that has OS/2 files or files used for the DOS session of OS/2, the partition can no longer be used by OS/2.

Note: *The PC DOS programs have been updated since the release of Windows 3.1. If you install Windows after installing PC DOS, check your CONFIG.SYS and AUTOEXEC.BAT files to make sure that you are using the programs HIMEM.SYS, EMM386.EXE, and SMARTDRV.EXE from the DOS directory and not the Windows directory.*

Steps To Take Before Using SuperStor/DS

Before running SuperStor/DS for the first time, you should create a bootable SuperStor/DS diskette that you can use to start your system in case of problems.

To create a bootable SuperStor/DS diskette, follow these steps:

1. Insert a blank, unformatted diskette into drive A.

2. At the PC DOS prompt, type **FORMAT A: /S /U**, and press **Enter**. PC DOS formats the diskette in drive A and copies the system files onto it.

3. Copy the following files from your hard disk to the diskette in drive A. (For information on copying files, see Chapter 1, "Understanding System Basics.")

   CONFIG.SYS

   DOS\DBLSPACE.BIN

   DOS\E.EXE

   DOS\E.EX

   DOS\ATTRIB.EXE

   DOS\CHKDSK.COM

   DOS\RTOOL.EXE

   DOS\DEFRAG.EXE

   DOS\FORMAT.COM

DOS\SSTOR.EXE

DOS\SSUTIL.EXE

DOS\SSUNCOMP.EXE

Note: *If all the files will not fit on one diskette, repeat steps 1 and 2 to create another formatted diskette. Then copy the remaining files onto the second diskette.*

4. Edit the CONFIG.SYS file on the diskette so that it contains only the following statement:

```
files=30
```

(For information on editing the CONFIG.SYS file, see Chapter 7, "Working with the Text Editor."

5. Turn your computer off and then on again so that it can boot from the diskette in drive A. At the A> prompt, type **C:** and press **Enter** to change to drive C. Start any program—just to make sure that you can access the files on drive C. Then remove the diskette from drive A and reboot your computer.

6. Store the diskette in a safe place.

Following are other actions you should take before using SuperStor/DS:

■ Delete unwanted files from the disk you are going to compress.

■ Make backups of your data files before you compress them.

■ Run CHKDSK on your drive to determine whether the disk has any errors that might cause the running of SuperStor/DS to fail. If the CHKDSK program finds errors, you should use the /F switch with CHKDSK to correct them. Continue to run CHKDSK until no errors are found. (For information on using CHKDSK, see Appendix A, "The PC DOS Top Twenty.")

■ Disable any programs, such as terminate-and-stay-resident programs (TSRs) that might interfere or cause problems while running SuperStor/DS. Then restart your system by pressing **Ctrl+Alt+Del**. Consult Appendix B, "Compatibility Considerations Regarding SuperStor/DS," for more information.

■ PC DOS allows you to have only one compression program on your system at a time. If you are changing to SuperStor/DS from another data compression program, make sure that you have uncompressed your data files and removed your current compression program.

Compressing a Drive Using the SuperStor/DS Prepare Command

The first time you run SuperStor/DS, you must prepare your DOS drive, using the Prepare command of the utility program. This document assumes that most people want to compress the entire disk on drive C. You can use the same procedure described here to prepare any drive for data compression.

To prepare your drive for data compression, follow these steps:

1. Exit Windows or any shell program that has a task swapper running before entering the SSTOR command.

2. Make sure that the following programs that interfere with Prepare are not loaded:

FASTOPEN

SHARE

DATAMON

3. Make sure that you are not using files or drives that have been created using one of the following PC DOS commands:

APPEND

ASSIGN

JOIN

SUBST

11

4. Run the PC DOS Defragmenter before you start SuperStor/DS. For information on using the PC DOS Defragmenter, see Chapter 10, "Using IBM Tools."

5. At the PC DOS command prompt, type **SSTOR** to start the SuperStor/DS program. The SuperStor/DS program appears on-screen.

A list of drives appears here

SuperStor/DS displays a main menu and a system device list. The system device list includes all the drives on your system that DOS recognizes.

Choose menu commands here

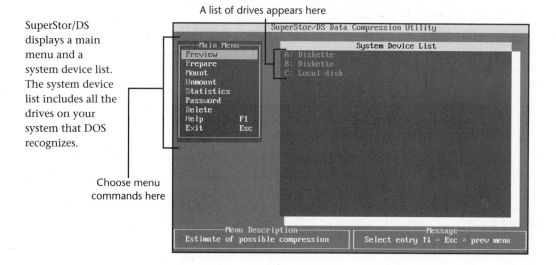

Note: *To choose a command in the SuperStor/DS utility program, use the arrow keys to highlight a command, and then press **Enter**. Press **Esc** to return to the previous screen.*

6. Choose **P**repare from the Main Menu. A Choose dialog box appears.

In the Choose dialog box, you can select the type of disk or space you want to prepare for compression.

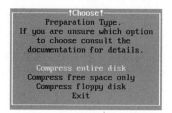

If you have problems...

If you see a message indicating that SuperStor/DS data compression is not enabled on your system, you have not yet run Prepare for the first time. If you have not run Prepare, press **N** to return to the SuperStor/DS screen. If you have run Prepare but have not rebooted, press **Y** to reboot your computer and enable SuperStor/DS. Then start again.

7. Choose Compress Entire Disk. Another Choose dialog box listing the available drives appears.

Specify the drive you want to compress.

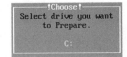

8. Enter the letter of the drive you want to compress. SuperStor/DS checks the drive for available space and other system requirements. It displays the Choose Ratio dialog box.

If you have problems...

If you see a message indicating that your computer does not have enough free space to compress the drive, you must delete unused files to make more space available. (You will need 1M of free space.) Press **Esc** to return to the SuperStor/DS screen, and then press **Esc** again to exit the program. Press **Y** and **Enter** to return to the PC DOS command prompt.

9. Choose Use Standard Ratio (2:1).

   Note: *The standard ratio option is designed for compressing data files that are a mixture of file types, such as program files, graphics files, and so on. If your files are usually a particular type of file that can be compressed at a higher ratio, you can choose Choose Compression Ratio, and specify a compression ratio of up to 8:1. You can use the SuperSTOR Preview command to determine a suggested ratio.*

10. If you selected the option Choose Compression Ratio, select a compression ratio of up to 8:1 from the list provided.

11. In the next dialog box, enter the number of megabytes of uncompressed space you want to reserve.

Note: *If you reserve space, that space is considered a separate, uncompressed drive and is named with the next available drive letter, such as drive D. Reserving space enables you to transfer from a compressed drive to an uncompressed drive programs that do not run well when compressed.*

12. In the next dialog box, select the drive letter to use when you are accessing the uncompressed drive created using the reserved space.

Prepare begins to compress your data files and to create a compressed volume file on the compressed disk. Then Prepare begins defragmenting your compressed volume file.

When Prepare is finished, it displays the following message:

```
Prepare has completed. Press any key to continue.
```

13. Press any key to return to the SuperStor/DS screen.

Caution
You cannot use Ctrl+Alt+Del or Esc while Prepare is running.

14. Press **Esc** to exit the SuperStor/DS utility. SuperStor/DS asks you to confirm that you want to exit. Press **Y** and then press **Enter** to return to the PC DOS command prompt.

15. Reboot your system to automount the compressed drives.

Compressing Diskettes

You can use SuperStor/DS to compress floppy diskettes as well as hard disks. Simply choose the diskette drive when running Prepare, as described in the previous section.

■ If you choose to compress a diskette in either drive A or drive B, you can use SuperStor/DS's UDE option. UDE prepares compressed data in a form that enables the data to be accessed from systems that do not have SuperStor/DS installed. Then, if you take the diskette to another computer, you can use it to read and write data, even if the other computer does not have SuperStor/DS installed.

■ To use a UDE disk on a computer that does not have SuperStor/DS, follow these steps:

1. Insert the UDE disk into the computer drive you want to use.

2. Run UDEON.COM from either drive A or drive B to install a limited version of the device driver. If you insert the UDE disk in drive A, for example, you type the following:

   A:UDEON

   Note: *You cannot start the UDEON.COM command from Windows or from the DOS session of OS/2 2.x.*

   Subsequent references to the diskette are now to any CVF on the diskette. Whether a UDE diskette is inserted in the drive or any other compressed diskette is inserted, the UDEON program remains active.

   With this program active, similar to fixed disks, your data is uncompressed as it is read from the diskette and compressed as it is written to the diskette if there is a DLBSPACE.*nnn* file on the diskette.

3. When you no longer need to use the compressed diskette, type the following, assuming again that you have the UDE disk in drive A:

   A:UDEOFF

   Running the program UDEOFF.COM removes the device driver and frees the memory the program was occupying.

■ You also can copy compressed files to a diskette that has not been prepared. The files are uncompressed as they are copied to the diskette.

The PC DOS Top Twenty

Although you may never use more than ten commands, PC DOS recognizes and responds to dozens of them. Use this section to familiarize yourself with twenty of the most common and useful PC DOS commands.

The most common PC DOS commands are built into the command processor (COMMAND.COM) and are instantly available at the system command prompt.

If you have problems...

If you try to enter a command, but PC DOS responds with the message Bad command or filename, you may need to specify the path to the command program file. You can change to the directory that holds the command (usually \DOS); you can include the path name every time you type the command; or you can add a PATH statement to your AUTOEXEC.BAT file. For more information about typing commands at the command prompt, see Chapter 1, "Understanding System Basics." For more information about the PATH command, see Chapter 2, "Making PC DOS Work." For more information about modifying your AUTOEXEC.BAT file, see Chapter 8, "Configuring Your Personal Computer."

In this section, each command is presented in the same format:

- *The command name.*

- *The command's purpose.*

- *The syntax.* The required format for entering the command. Parts of the syntax that you must enter are printed in boldface type; parts of the command that are optional are printed in italic type.

In the syntax, you must substitute specific information for some optional parameters: *d:* is the name of the disk drive holding the file, and *path* is the directory path to the file; *filename* is the name of the file, and *ext* is the file name extension. Commands that use source and destination drive parameters use *sd:* for the source drive name and *dd:* for the destination drive name. If any part of this notation does not appear in the syntax for the command, do not include the omitted part in the command.

■ *Step-by-step instructions* for using the command.

■ *Cautions, tips, or notes* about the command, often including a brief comment indicating the emphasis you should place on mastering the command.

CD or CHDIR

Purpose

Use CHDIR or CD for the following tasks:

■ Change the current directory

■ Show the name of the current directory

Syntax

CD *d:path*

or

CHDIR *d:path*

Steps

To use CD or CHDIR, follow these steps:

1. Type **CD** or **CHDIR**.

2. Press the **spacebar** once.

3. Type the path to the directory to which you want to change. Remember to use the backslash to separate the parts of the path.

Note: *Do not type a path if you want to show the name of the current directory.*

4. Press **Enter**.

CD or CHDIR is important and simple to use; it is one of the commands you need so that you can navigate around your disk.

CHKDSK

Purpose

Use CHKDSK for the following tasks:

- Check the directory for disk and memory status. CHKDSK displays the following information:

    Number of files and directories on a disk

    Number of bytes used and the space available on a disk

    The number of hidden files

    The information that a diskette is (or is not) bootable

    The total bytes and bytes free

- Make minor repairs

Syntax

CHKDSK *d:path\filename.ext /switches*

Steps

To use CHKDSK, follow these steps:

1. Type **CHKDSK**, and press the **spacebar** once. You may need to precede the command with the drive name and path because CHKDSK is an external command.

2. To check a disk on another drive, type the drive name, followed by a colon (:), after CHKDSK. For example, if your default drive is C and you want to check drive B, type **CHKDSK B:** at the PC DOS command prompt.

3. You can use CHKDSK to determine the fragmented areas in an individual file by entering the path, file name, and extension. The file name and extension can contain wild cards.

4. Press **Enter**.

CHKDSK gives you control of your computer. This simple command provides a quick analysis for your diskettes and hard disks. You should use it regularly.

Note: *For more information about the switches you can use with this command, type HELP CHKDSK.*

COPY

Purpose

Use COPY for the following tasks:

- Copy one or more files to another disk or directory, or copy a file to the same directory and change its name

- Transfer information between PC DOS system devices

- Send text to the printer

- Create ASCII text files and batch files

Syntax

The most common syntax for the COPY command is

COPY *sd:\spath\sfilename.ext dd:\dpath\dfilename.ext /v*

Steps

To use COPY, follow these steps:

1. Type **COPY**, and press the **spacebar** once.

2. Type the drive name and path of the source file (*sd:\spath*).

3. Type the name of the file you want to copy. You can use wild cards.

4. Press the **spacebar** once.

5. Type the drive name, path, and file name of the target file (*dd:\dpath*). Skip this step if the destination file name is to remain the same as that of the source file.

6. You also can add the /V switch to verify and check the accuracy of the COPY procedure.

7. Press **Enter**.

Note: *If you try to copy a file into a directory where a file with the same name already exists, PC DOS prompts you to confirm that you want to overwrite the existing file.*

Note: *For information about additional switches you can use with this command, type HELP COPY.*

DATE

Purpose

Use DATE for the following tasks:

- Enter or change the system date which sets the internal clock on a computer

- Check the current date for new and modified files

- Provide control for programs that require date information

Syntax

DATE *mm-dd-yy*

Steps

To use DATE, follow these steps:

1. Type **DATE**, and press the **spacebar** once.

2. Enter the date in the following format:

    mm-dd-yy

    mm is a one- or two-digit number for the month (1 through 12).

dd is a one- or two-digit number for the day (1 through 31).

yy is a one- or two-digit number for the year (80 through 99). PC DOS assumes that the first two digits of the year are *19*.

Note: *You can separate the entries with hyphens, periods, or slashes.*

3. Press **Enter**.

If your computer does not have a built-in calendar clock, use DATE every time you boot. Knowing when files were written or updated is good organizational strategy and aids you in being selective with CPBACKUP and XCOPY.

DEL

Purpose

Use DEL for the following task:

Remove one or more files from the current disk or directory

Syntax

DEL *d:path\filename.ext /P*

Steps

To use DEL, follow these steps:

Caution

DEL is a deceptively simple command that can make your life easy or fill it with grief. Think carefully before you press Enter.

1. Type **DEL**, and press the **spacebar** once.

2. Type the drive name and path of the file you want to delete, unless the file is in the current directory.

3. Type the name of the file you want to delete.

4. You can use the following switch:

/P prompts `filename Delete (Y/N)?` before each file is deleted. Press **Y** to delete the file or **N** to cancel the command.

5. Press **Enter**.

Note: *Be very careful when you use wild cards, or you may delete more files than you intend. If necessary, you may be able to recover deleted files by using the UNDELETE command. See Chapter 10, "Using IBM Tools," for more information.*

Note: *For information about additional switches you can use with this command, type HELP DEL.*

DIR

Purpose

Use DIR for the following tasks:

- Display a list of files and subdirectories in a disk's directory

- List a specified group of files within a directory

- Examine the volume identification label of the disk

- Determine the amount of available space on the disk

- Check the size of individual files

- Check the date the files were last modified

Syntax

DIR *d:\path\filename.ext /switches*

Steps

To use DIR, follow these steps:

1. Type **DIR**, and press the **spacebar** once.

2. You also can type one of the following:

    The drive name of the directory you want to display.

    The path name of the directory you want to display.

    The file name, if you want to limit the number and types of files listed. You can use wild cards to list groups of files.

3. You can use any of the following switches:

/W displays the directory in a wide format of five columns across. The /W switch displays only the directory name and file names. For large listings, also include the /P switch.

/P displays the directory and pauses between screen pages. This switch prevents large directories from scrolling off the screen before you can read them.

/O *sort* displays files in sorted order, as in /OE. The sort options are as follows:

N sorts in alphabetical order by file name.

E sorts in alphabetical order by extension.

D sorts by date and time, earliest to latest.

S sorts by size, smallest to largest.

C sorts by compression ratio, lowest to highest.

G lists directories before file names.

–*sort* sorts in reverse order.

4. Press **Enter**.

DISKCOPY

Purpose

Use DISKCOPY for the following task:

Duplicate a diskette.

Note: *DISKCOPY works only when copying disks of the same size and capacity*

Syntax

DISKCOPY *sd: dd: /switches*

Steps

To use DISKCOPY, follow these steps:

Caution

If a problem exists on the original (source) diskette, the same problem will appear on the duplicate diskette.

1. Type **DISKCOPY**, and press the **spacebar** once.

2. Type the name of the drive that holds the source (original) disk and a colon (A:, for example). Press the **spacebar** again.

3. Type the name of the drive that holds the target (new) disk and a colon (B:, for example).

4. Press **Enter**. Within a few seconds, PC DOS prompts you to place the source disk into drive A and the target disk into drive B. If you have only one diskette drive, PC DOS prompts you to place the source disk into drive A.

5. Insert the requested diskette(s), and press **Enter**. If you have only one diskette drive, PC DOS prompts you (as many times as necessary) to exchange the source disk with the target disk.

6. When the copy is complete, PC DOS asks whether you want to copy another diskette.

7. Press **Y**, and repeat steps 6 through 8 to copy another disk; otherwise, press **N**.

DOSSHELL

Purpose

Use DOSSHELL for the following tasks:

- Perform PC DOS commands from a graphical interface
- Manage files and directories
- Manage and start programs

Syntax

DOSSHELL

Steps

To use DOSSHELL, follow these steps:

1. Type **DOSSHELL**. You may need to precede the command with the drive name and path for DOSSHELL.COM because DOSSHELL is an external command.

2. Press **Enter**.

This command can be placed in the AUTOEXEC.BAT file.

FORMAT

Purpose

Use FORMAT for the following task:

Caution
FORMAT should be used carefully. When you use this command, all files are erased.

Prepare a diskette or hard disk to accept PC DOS information

Syntax

FORMAT *d: /switches*

Steps

To use FORMAT, follow these steps:

1. Type **FORMAT**.

2. Press the **spacebar** once.

3. Type the name of the drive holding the disk you want to format and a colon (for example, A:).

4. If necessary, use the /F:*size* switch to format a diskette to a specific capacity, where *size* is one of the following values: 160, 180, 320, 360, 720, 1.2, 1.44, or 2.88.

   If you format a 360K diskette in a 1.2M disk drive, the formatted disk will not be readable unless formatted for a 360K drive using the /F switch. Also, a 1.2M disk may look exactly like a 360K diskette, but you cannot use the higher density 1.2M diskette in a 360K disk drive.

5. Press **Enter**.

6. PC DOS now instructs you to place a diskette into the drive you named in step 3. Insert the diskette you want to format, and press **Enter**.

In a few minutes, you see the message Format complete and a status report of the formatted disk. PC DOS then prompts you to enter a label name.

7. Type a label name of no more than 11 characters and press Enter, or just press Enter for no label name. PC DOS asks whether you want to format another disk.

8. Press **Y** and repeat steps 6 and 7 to format another disk; otherwise, press **N**.

You absolutely must understand FORMAT. This command is the heart of your disk maintenance system. If you accidentally format an already formatted disk, you may be able to recover the information by using the UNFORMAT command.

Note: *For information about the switches you can use with this command, type HELP FORMAT.*

HELP

Purpose

Use HELP for the following task:

Display syntax for a command

Syntax

HELP *command*

Steps

To use HELP, follow these steps:

1. Type **HELP**, and press the **spacebar** once. You might need to precede the command with the drive name and path for HELP.EXE because HELP is an external command.

2. Type the command for which you want to get help (for example, FORMAT). If you do not enter a command name, HELP displays a complete listing of all the commands with a brief description of each.

3. Press **Enter**.

MD or MKDIR

Purpose

Use MD or MKDIR for the following task:

Create subdirectories to help organize your files

Syntax

MD *d:path\directory*

or

MKDIR *d:path\directory*

Steps

To use MD or MKDIR, follow these steps:

1. Type **MD** or **MKDIR**, and press the **spacebar** once.

2. If necessary, type the drive name and path of the new directory.

3. Type the directory name.

4. Press **Enter**.

If you have a hard disk drive, you need to understand this command.

MORE

Purpose

Use MORE in conjunction with commands for the following task:

Display data one screen at a time

Syntax

TYPE *d:path\filename.ext* ¦ **MORE**

Steps

To use MORE with the TYPE command, for example, follow these steps:

1. Type **TYPE filename.ext ¦ MORE**, and press **Enter**.

The displayed information pauses when the screen is full, and PC DOS displays the following message

—More—

2. Press any key to display the next page of data.

MORE is convenient for reading files longer than one screen. You can cancel the MORE by using CTRL+Break.

Tip
The ¦ is an uppercase \.

PATH

Purpose

Use PATH for the following task:

Access files not in the default directory without changing directories. PATH tells PC DOS to search specified directories on specified drives if it does not find a program or batch file in the current directory. (The maximum length of the path cannot exceed 127 characters.)

Syntax

> **PATH** *d1:\path1;d2:\path2;d3:\path3;...*

Steps

To use PATH, follow these steps:

1. Type **PATH**, and press the **spacebar** once.

2. Type the drive name you want to include in the search path (for example, A:, B:, or C:). If you include the drive name with the path, PC DOS finds your files even if you change default drives.

3. Type the directory path you want to search (for example, \KEEP).

4. To add another directory to the search path, type a semicolon (;), and then type the drive name and path of the additional directory.

5. Repeat steps 2 through 4 until you type all the subdirectory paths you want PC DOS to search.

6. Press **Enter**.

PATH is an important navigational aid you should understand fully. If you do not understand PATH, you may not understand the directory concept.

PRINT

Purpose

Use PRINT for the following tasks:

- Print a text file while you are using other IBM PC DOS commands

- Display the contents of the print queue

Syntax

> **PRINT** *d:path\directory\filename.ext /switches*

Steps

To use PRINT, follow these steps:

1. Type **PRINT**, and press the **spacebar**. You may need to precede the command with the drive name and path if PRINT is not in the current directory or in a path governed by the PATH command.

2. Type the drive name, path, and file name of the file you want to print.

3. You can use any of the following switches:

   /C cancels printing of the preceding file name and subsequent file names.

   /P adds the preceding file name and subsequent file names to the print queue.

4. The first time you use PRINT, PC DOS displays this message:

   ```
   NAME of list device [PRN]:
   ```

   Just press Enter to continue. The default printer device LPT1 will be used.

5. Press **Enter**.

Tip

Use PRINT without parameters to display the contents of the print queue.

PROMPT

Purpose

Use PROMPT for the following tasks:

- Customize the PC DOS system command prompt

- Display the drive and directory path

- Display a message on-screen

- Display the date and time or the PC DOS version number

Syntax

PROMPT *string*

Steps

To use PROMPT, follow these steps:

1. Type **PROMPT**, and press the **spacebar** once.

2. Type the text string and the arrangement of parameters you want to display.

3. You can use the following characters, preceded by a dollar sign ($), with the PROMPT command to produce your own PC DOS command prompt:

$D displays the current date.

$G displays the > character.

$L displays the < character.

$N displays the current disk drive name.

$P displays the current drive and path.

$T displays the system time.

$E displays a left arrow.

$_ moves the cursor to the beginning of the next line.

PROMPT is used most frequently to extend the visual command line to display the path of your resident directory.

RD or RMDIR

Purpose

Use RD or RMDIR for the following task:

Remove a directory

Syntax

> **RD** *d:path*

or

> **RMDIR** *d:path*

Steps

To use RD or RMDIR, follow these steps:

Caution
You cannot remove the current directory or root directory. You must change to the directory containing the directory you want to remove before you try to remove it.

1. Use the DEL command to delete all files from the directory you want to remove.

2. Change to the directory that contains the directory you want to remove.

3. Type **RD** or **RMDIR**, and press the **spacebar** once.

4. Type the full path and name of the directory you want to remove.

5. Press **Enter**.

RD or RMDIR is another essential command for maintaining a logical hard disk drive subdirectory system.

REN or RENAME

Purpose

Use REN or RENAME for the following task:

> Change the file name or extension of a file or group of files (using wild-card characters ? and #)

Syntax

> **REN** *d:path\old filename.ext newfilename.ext*

> **RENAME** *d:path\oldfilename.ext newfilename.ext*

Steps

To use REN or RENAME, follow these steps:

1. Type **REN** or **RENAME**, and press the **spacebar** once.

2. Type the drive name and path of the file you want to rename.

Caution
Avoid giving files in different directories the same file name. You might accidentally delete the wrong file.

3. Type the name of the file you want to rename. You can use wild cards (* and ?) to specify groups of files.

4. Press the **spacebar**.

5. Type the new name you want to assign the file, and press **Enter**.

This command can be very helpful.

Tip

You can rename files only from within the current directory.

TIME

Purpose

Use TIME for the following tasks:

- Enter or change the time used by the system which sets the automatic clock on a computer

- Establish the time that files were created or modified

- Provide control for programs that require time information

Syntax

TIME *hh:mm:ss.xx a\p*

Steps

To use TIME, follow these steps:

1. Type **TIME**, and press the **spacebar** once.

2. Enter the time in the format *hh:mm:ss:xx* or *hh.mm.ss.xx*.

For *hh*, type the hour, using one or two digits from 0 through 3. For *mm*, type the number of minutes, using one or two digits from 0 through 59. For *ss*, type the number of seconds, using one or two digits from 0 through 59. For *xx*, type the number of hundredths of a second, using one or two digits from 0 through 99. It is not necessary to include more than the hour and the minutes, however.

3. If you want to use the 12-hour clock when you enter the time, type **a** to represent a.m. or **p** to represent p.m. For the 24-hour clock, omit these identifiers. (For example, to indicate 3:13 p.m., type **3:13p** for the 12-hour clock or **15:13** for the 24-hour clock.)

4. Press **Enter**.

It's a good idea to use TIME with the DATE command. Including the correct time in a file may not be as important as including the date, but having the time can be helpful.

TYPE

Purpose

Use TYPE for the following tasks:

- Display the contents of a text file on-screen

- Send files to the printer

Syntax

TYPE *d:path\filename.ext*

Steps

To use TYPE, follow these steps:

1. Type **TYPE**, and press the **spacebar** once.

2. Type the drive name, path, and file name of the file you want to display.

3. Press **Enter**.

To send the typed output to a device such as the printer (PRN), use the redirection symbol >, as shown in this example:

TYPE TEXT.TXT > PRN

TYPE enables you to read an ASCII text file without opening it in a word processing program.

XCOPY

Purpose

Use XCOPY for the following tasks:

- Copy files from multiple directories to another disk

- Copy files with a specific date

- Copy new or modified files

- Copy subdirectories and files

Syntax

XCOPY *sd:spath\sfilename.ext dd:dpath\dfilename.ext /switches*

Steps

To use XCOPY, follow these steps:

Caution
Before you use XCOPY, make sure that you have typed the correct information so that you do not accidentally copy over important files.

1. Type **XCOPY**, and press the **spacebar** once. You may need to precede the command with the drive name and path for XCOPY.EXE because XCOPY is an external command.

2. Type the drive name and path of the source file (*sd:\spath*), if necessary.

3. Type the name of the file you want to copy. You can use wild cards.

4. Press the **spacebar**.

5. Type the drive name, path, and file name of the target file (*dd:\dpath\dfilename.ext*).

6. You can use any of the following switches:

/D:date copies files that were created or modified on or after the specified date.

/P prompts you before copying each file.

/S copies specified files from the current directory and from subdirectories of the current directory, creating directories on the destination disk when necessary.

/E copies empty subdirectories.

/V verifies each copied file.

/W makes XCOPY wait before starting the copy so that you can insert the correct disks in the drive.

7. Press **Enter**.

A

Appendix B

Compatibility Considerations Regarding SuperStor/DS

Many manufacturers supply hardware and software for your computer. Some products you buy for your computer may not work properly together, however. This section lists products that are not compatible with SuperStor/DS, the PC DOS data compression program, as of this writing, or that have certain features that are not compatible.

Most programs and utilities built into PC DOS are compatible with the SuperStor/DS data compression program, but there are some exceptions. For more information about SuperStor/DS and data compression, see Chapter 11, "Using Data Compression."

PC DOS Program	Usage Restrictions
APPEND	Do not use compression on an appended directory.
ASSIGN	Do not use compression on a drive that was created using the ASSIGN command.
DATAMON	Turn off this program when you are compressing or uncompressing.
FASTOPEN	Disable this program before compressing.
JOIN	Do not use compression on drives that have been created with the JOIN command.
SHARE	Do not use compression on files using the SHARE program.
SUBST	Do not use compression on a drive letter when you have used the SUBST command to assign the drive letter to a directory.

The following chart lists other programs that are known to be incompatible with SuperStor/DS.

Incompatible Program	Type
MS-DOS	Operating system
Client-server network system	Network system

Norton Utilities prior to Version 7
    Disk Doctor
    NCACHE
    Speedisk
	Disk utility programs

OS/2	Operating system

PC TOOLS Deluxe, prior to Version 8.0
    Compress Disk
    Disk Fix
    Mirror
	Disk utility programs

QEMM NOXMS parameter	Memory management program
QRAM NOAUTO parameter	Memory management program
SpaceManager	Data compression program
SpinRite prior to Version 3.1	Disk utility program
Stacker 3.0	Data compression program
Stacker 3.1	Data compression program
SuperStor 2.0	Data compression program
SuperStor PRO	Data compression program
WD-7000 FASST	Hardware disk-caching program

Note: *The README.TXT file on the PC DOS 6.3 Setup diskette 1 contains additional information that became available after this book was published.*

If you have problems...   If you elect to use third-party programs, use only defragmenting, disk-repairing, and other disk utilities that explicitly claim compatibility with SuperStor/DS or Microsoft DoubleSpace.

Using SuperStor/DS with Other Data Compression Programs

You should use only one compression program at one time.

If you want to use SpaceManager with PC DOS Compression, you must take one of the following precautionary measures:

- Add the NOAUTO parameter to the ADDSTOR.INI file.

- Do not run SMOUNT.EXE.

Note: *SMOUNT.EXE is set up to run by default by SpaceManager. Refer to the SpaceManager documentation for information on changing defaults.*

If you have another data compression program installed (including SuperStor 2.0 or SuperStor PRO), you can continue to use your current compression program. You may, however, want to uncompress your files and remove your present data compression program and use SuperStor/DS instead because SuperStor/DS is specifically designed to work with PC DOS 6.3.

See Chapter 11, "Using Data Compression," for information about removing other compression programs if you want to remove Microsoft DoubleSpace, Stacker 3.0 or 3.1, or previous versions of SuperStor.

Using SuperStor/DS with Disk Utility Programs

PC DOS provides its own disk utility programs—sometimes known as disk-optimizing programs, disk-repairing utilities, disk-caching programs, and disk-partitioning programs—that are compatible with SuperStor/DS.

Some disk utility programs provided by third-party suppliers bypass normal PC DOS file operations and directly modify the disk's File Allocation Table (FAT) or other internal control information. Because SuperStor/DS maintains its own internal file structures, some features of these programs may not work properly on a SuperStor/DS disk.

B

Watch out for utilities that provide the following functions:

- Recalibration

- Realignment

- Formatting

- Unformatting

- Repair of the FAT or other parts of the disk

- Defragmentation

Utility programs that depend on the physical characteristics of the hardware or access the hardware directly generally do not work with SuperStor/DS. You cannot run such programs on your SuperStor/DS disk, but you can run them on the uncompressed portion of your disk. For example, you can run these utilities on the host drive that contains the compressed volume file (CVF). However, you should *never* use any such program to repair your compressed volume file.

If you have questions about how a disk utility program functions, contact the software provider.

Using SuperStor/DS with Deletion-Protection Programs

Utility programs that provide deletion protection are compatible with SuperStor/DS during normal operations. However, you should turn these off by using the PC DOS REM command while you prepare your SuperStor/DS disk.

SSUTIL's SHRINK DISK can fail if it finds hidden fixed files, such as the Delete Sentry directories on both the compressed and the host drives. Do not use SHRINK DISK if you have deletion-protection software products unless you delete the Delete Sentry directories.

Note: *You should turn off third-party deletion-protection programs before preparing your disk.*

Using SuperStor/DS with Memory Managers

SuperStor/DS is compatible with most popular memory-management software products.

QEMM or QRAM

Caution
Do not use the NOXMS parameter with QEMM.
Do not use the NOAUTO parameter with QRAM.

SuperStor/DS is compatible with QEMM or QRAM. You must use the NOUMB parameter when loading the DBLSPACE.SYS driver or using ST_DBL.SYS from QEMM Version 7.0 when you use one of these memory managers.

If QEMM loads the SuperStor/DS device driver completely into upper memory, you cannot use SMARTDRV.EXE from your AUTOEXEC.BAT. You must disable the call to it and restart your computer before running OPTIMIZE. This problem does not exist for other memory managers or other disk caches. Nor is there a problem with SMARTDRV.SYS, which is included with Windows 3.0 or PC DOS 5.0 versions.

386MAX or BlueMAX

If you are using Version 7.0 of 386MAX or BlueMAX, do not use the following statement in your CONFIG.SYS file:

```
DEVICE=DBLSPACE.SYS
```

Version 7.0 of these memory managers moves the driver; Version 6.0 does not move the driver.

Using SuperStor/DS on Networks

SuperStor/DS is not designed to work with network servers in client/server environments. You should not try to install SuperStor/DS on a server in such an environment.

SuperStor/DS is compatible with most network drivers on the client side of the network, but you should not try to turn a network volume into a SuperStor/DS disk. SuperStor/DS can manage a disk only on the computer on which you have installed it.

B

Before installing SuperStor/DS on a network, you should discuss the situation with your network administrator. SuperStor/DS should coexist with most peer-to-peer network environments that run under PC DOS. Be careful, however, not to remap a network drive over a drive letter in use by SuperStor/DS.

Using SuperStor/DS with Other Hardware and Software under PC DOS

SuperStor/DS has been tested extensively with products from many suppliers. This section discusses compatibility with specific software and hardware products.

Laptop Computers

You can use SuperStor/DS safely on a laptop computer. However, during the Prepare option of SuperStor/DS, use your AC adapter. Using your laptop's AC adapter prevents interruptions caused by weak or failing batteries. You should always use your laptop's AC adapter when you run the SuperStor/DS utility programs ANALYSIS and DISK TUNEUP.

Bernoulli Hardware Driver

DOSAOD.SYS is the Bernoulli hardware driver. For a Bernoulli drive to automount, you must manually mount it once. After the Bernoulli has been mounted once, it automounts thereafter.

SpinRite

Versions of SpinRite prior to version 3.1 are not compatible with SuperStor/DS.

WD-7000 FASST

You cannot use WD-7000 FASST with SuperStor/DS.

Using SuperStor/DS with the OS/2 Operating System

SuperStor/DS is not compatible with OS/2. You cannot use SuperStor/DS to compress data on a partition that contains OS/2. When you use SuperStor/DS and compress data on a partition that is shared by OS/2 and PC DOS (such as dual-boot or multi-boot systems), the partition can no longer be used by OS/2.

Using SuperStor/DS with Task-Switching Program Managers

Caution
Do not run the SuperStor/DS utility programs from IBM DOS Shell with Task Swapper running, from within the Windows Program Manager, or from any other shell program with a task-switching system.

Task-switching program managers, such as Microsoft Windows or shell programs, are programs that extend the PC DOS operating environment by providing task-switching or program-switching capabilities.

Never install SuperStor/DS under a task-switching system. Always invoke the SuperStor/DS commands SSTOR and SSUTIL from the PC DOS command prompt or after a complete exit from the task-switching program manager.

B

Index

X

To order additional copies of this book:

Call 1-800-428-5331
or write:

Macmillan Computer Publishing

201 W. 103rd Street

Indianapolis, IN 46290-1097

Please refer to the source code PCDS.